Treat Her Like Your Child and She'll Marry You

MAURICE COLE

This is a work of nonfiction. Some names and identifying details may have been changed to protect privacy.

Unless otherwise indicated, Scripture quotations are taken from the King James Version (KJV) of the Bible, which is in the public domain.

The author acknowledges the influence of the following works:
Chop Wood Carry Water by Joshua Medcalf
The Five Love Languages by Gary Chapman
The Holy Bible (KJV)

Copyright © 2025 by Maurice Cole
Published by ColeVision LLC
ISBN: Paperback: 979-8-9991832-0-0 | Hardback: 979-8-9991832-1-7 | Ebook: 979-8-9991832-2-4

First Edition
June 2025

For more information or permissions, visit: **lovethatstays.com**

To my wife, Marina Cole.
You've loved me at my worst, and you've loved me at my best.
Greatness isn't easy — but you give me a reason to chase it every single day.
I love you.

Treat Her Like Your Child and She'll Marry You

MAURICE COLE

CONTENTS

INTRO

"Treat Her Like Your Child, and She'll Marry You" – A Thought-Provoking Perspective

The title itself sparks strong reactions. At first glance, the phrase "like your child" can trigger alarm bells, leading some to dismiss the concept without hearing the explanation. But when you pause, reflect, and truly consider the idea, there's profound wisdom in this approach. The truth is, there are elements of how we treat our children that would revolutionize romantic relationships if applied intentionally and consistently.

The Core Idea

Imagine the way a loving parent treats their child. They love them unconditionally, protect them fiercely, nurture their growth, and ensure they feel valued and cherished. Who wouldn't want to experience that in a relationship? While romantic partners are, of course, not children, the principles of care, attention, and devotion are universally desired.

Many times, relationships become overly complicated when simple, foundational principles are ignored. Men, by adopting the mindset of caring for your partner as you would a beloved child—not in a patronizing way, but with the same level of commitment, love, and patience—you can unlock deeper emotional intimacy and trust.

For the Skeptics

Some women may think, *"I'm not a child, and I don't want to be treated as one!"* And they're right—not in the literal sense. But think about this: Would you ever do something to your child that would make them feel unworthy or insignificant? Quite the opposite. Most parents strive to empower their children, instilling confidence and making them feel like the center of their world. For many, their children are the highlight of their lives. Wouldn't you want to be the highlight of someone's life? To be treated with that same level of care, attention, and dedication?

The Biblical Blueprint

For believers, the foundation for this approach is rooted in Scripture. Christ gave husbands clear instructions: *"Husbands, love your wives, even as Christ also loved the church, and gave himself for it"* (Ephesians 5:25, KJV). Christ's love for the church—His "children"—is the epitome of selfless, unconditional love. He loved with a love that was sacrificial, forgiving, and without flaw.

While achieving Christ-like love is a tall order, it's not impossible. For those who trust in God, the strength and guidance to love your partner in this way are readily available. For non-believers, this principle still holds weight: treating your partner with unwavering love, respect, and care is a recipe for relational success.

The Blueprint for Non-Believers

Even outside the context of faith, the principles of unconditional love, protection, and care resonate universally. At the end of this book, there's a questionnaire that 99.9% of readers will answer affirmatively, aligning their desires with the foundational principles of this blueprint. For non-believers curious about what faith entails, the closing chapters will explore this concept further.

Equipping Men for Success

Men, by the time you finish this book, you'll have the tools necessary to become the kind of man women will want to marry—one who navigates the complexities of relationships with confidence and grace. While many of these principles may seem simple, the challenge lies in executing them consistently. Success in relationships doesn't come from grand gestures alone; it's about the daily commitment to love, patience, and intentional action.

This journey isn't just about learning—it's about transforming your approach to relationships and becoming the kind of partner who builds a love that lasts.

Let's dive in. And if something doesn't sit right with you, I'd love to hear your thoughts. Email me directly at **maurice.mcole@gmail.com**. I genuinely welcome the conversation.

WIFE TALK

SPEAKING HER LANGUAGE: COMMUNICATING WITH CARE

"Let your speech be always with grace, season with salt, that ye may know how ye ought to answer every man."

Have you ever seen a parent talking to their newborn baby? Often, they'll speak in "baby talk" with a soft, soothing voice designed to connect with and comfort their child. At that moment, the parent isn't worried about how they look to the outside world. The only thing that matters is the smile or laughter they can bring to their baby's face. Peekaboo, for example, is a classic game that rarely fails to light up a baby's world.

In the same way, we need to embrace "wife talk" when communicating with the woman we're dating or married to. No, this doesn't mean using Goo Goo or Ga Ga, but the approach is similar. The goal is to communicate in a way that resonates with her and makes her feel understood and valued. Men, by nature, often communicate in a direct, straightforward manner, which works fine with other men. However, with women, it's essential to wrap the message with care—layer it with "bubble wrap," so to speak.

Communication is as much about the person receiving the message as it is about the message itself. If someone only speaks Italian, you wouldn't relay a message in French and expect it to land. Similarly, with women, tapping into their emotions and presenting your message with sensitivity is key. For example, imagine your partner asking you how she looks in a particular outfit. If you don't find it flattering, you could say, "You look lovely, but I think the outfit you wore the other day was even more stunning." This response offers a compliment while gently redirecting the focus away from the current outfit.

What might seem like a simple yes-or-no question to you often carries more weight for her. She's not just asking for your opinion on the outfit; she's seeking validation and reassurance that you find her attractive. Your response is an opportunity to affirm her confidence and strengthen her trust in your bond. Effective communication in a relationship requires intention, empathy, and an understanding of how your words affect your partner emotionally. When you tailor your approach with care, you create a deeper connection that brings smiles and joy—not unlike that parent talking to their baby.

The Silent Language

A parent's warm smile, gentle touch, or open posture communicates safety and love, reassuring the child even in moments of uncertainty or distress. For instance, imagine a toddler who has fallen and is looking to their parent for a reaction. If the parent maintains calm body language—kneeling to their level, offering a gentle smile, and extending open arms—the child will likely feel secure and comforted. On the other hand, tense or dismissive body language can exacerbate the child's fear or confusion. The impact of something as simple as a reaction to an event can have lasting effects on a child's emotional development. Similarly, consider the dynamic in your relationship when your partner is trying to share a problem from their day, and you appear distracted—perhaps preoccupied with your phone, crossing your arms, or avoiding eye contact. Even if you are listening, your body language tells a different story, potentially leading to confusion or frustration for your partner.

It's crucial to remember that the emotions you evoke within your partner are just as important as the words you use in your response. Effective empathy requires not only understanding your partner's feelings and perspectives but also communicating that understanding through your actions.

If empathy is an area you struggle with, a good starting point is maintaining eye contact and adopting an open, welcoming posture. These nonverbal cues create the perception of a safe, supportive space. Coupled with a gentle and thoughtful verbal response, you significantly increase the likelihood of fostering a positive and productive conversation. Minor adjustments in your body language can transform the quality of your interactions and strengthen emotional connections.

"Only 7% of communication is verbal, while 93% is nonverbal. Your body language speaks volumes."
Albert Mehrabian

Post Me

In today's world, social media offers a unique opportunity to express affection and appreciation for the people we care about, especially in relationships. Sharing a post about your partner or sending them something thoughtful can be a simple yet impactful way to show how much they mean to you. A heartfelt caption, a sweet video, or a cherished memory shared online communicates, "I see you, I value you, and I'm not afraid to show it." However, it's essential to ensure this aligns with their comfort level—some people enjoy bold declarations, while others prefer subtler gestures.

Here are a few different ways to show you care:

1. **Create a "Then vs. Now" photo collage**

   ○ Highlight how your relationship has grown with captions that show your appreciation for her.

2. **Highlight her accomplishments**

   ○ Post about something she's achieved, like a new job, project, or personal goal, and write, "You never cease to amaze me!"

3. **Post a short video montage**

   ○ Compile clips of your favorite moments together and set to a song that reminds you of her.

The Bible teaches the value of boasting in the goodness of God: "Let the one who boasts boast in the Lord" (2 Corinthians 10:17). Similarly, celebrating those we care about reflects the love and joy God places in our lives. For instance, Proverbs 31:28 praises the virtuous woman, stating, "Her children arise and call her blessed; her husband also, and he praises her." Publicly or privately honoring someone special demonstrates gratitude for the blessing they are while giving glory to God.

When posting about her, make it personal. Share photos or videos that reflect her personality and joys, or send her something that will make her smile, like a funny meme or an encouraging message. Even small gestures like a "thinking of you" video or a playlist celebrating shared memories show that you're paying attention and value her uniqueness. These actions echo Romans 12:10: "Be devoted to one another in love. Honor one another above yourselves."

Ultimately, it's not about perfection but thoughtfulness. A simple "I'm grateful for you today" post or a private message saying how much she means to you can speak volumes. Social media can become a tool for modern love letters rooted in kindness and intentionality. By thoughtfully celebrating her, you strengthen your bond and mirror God's example of honoring and uplifting those we love, showcasing the beauty of love in its purest form.

Navigating the Challenges of Communication

Not every conversation will be as straightforward as discussing an outfit. There will be times when emotions run high, and effectively communicating will feel especially challenging. This is why counselors often advise parents not to discipline their children while angry—making logical decisions, not emotional ones, is crucial. The same principle applies when speaking with your partner. Taking the time to gather your thoughts before responding allows you to relay your message with love and intention rather than in the heat of frustration.

Tonality and volume are critical components of effective communication, especially within the context of relationships. Imagine walking into a room where the music is blaring at maximum volume. What's your immediate reaction? Most likely, your first concern is not what song is playing but rather how to turn the volume down or why it's so loud in the first place. The content of the music becomes irrelevant when the volume is overwhelming. Communication with your partner operates in much the same way. When emotions escalate and yelling takes over, the message is often lost, overshadowed by the intensity of delivery.

When we raise our voices, the substance of our message is frequently overlooked, and the person on the receiving end may feel diminished or disrespected. This dynamic creates a barrier to understanding, undermining the very goal of communication: connection and clarity. Effective communication requires that the message be delivered in a way that is easily digestible, much like preparing baby food. It takes time, care, and intentionality to deliver a message with love and compassion. Our tone can either build trust and intimacy or create distance and defensiveness.

YOU WOULDN'T FEED A BABY STEAK—SO WHY SERVE YOUR PARTNER A MESSAGE THAT'S HARD TO CHEW?

If you find yourself unable to communicate without raising your voice, it's a clear sign that you may not be in the right state of mind for a constructive conversation. Emotions often cloud judgment, driving communication in a direction that is counterproductive. In these moments, it's essential to pause, reflect, and regain composure before proceeding. When tone and volume are controlled, messages are more likely to be received with openness and understanding, fostering a healthier, more respectful dialogue.

A wise man once said, "You'll almost never regret the words you don't say in anger, but you'll often regret the harsh ones you do." Truth, when delivered without love, can leave scars—wounds that may heal on the surface but can leave lasting emotional damage beneath. While you may forget the words you spoke in the heat of the moment, your partner likely won't. Those words can echo in their mind, shaping how they feel about you and the relationship. Be mindful of the power of your words, and remember that love and kindness are the foundations of effective communication, even in moments of conflict.

Positive Affirmations

So, what can we actually say that makes an impact? Positive affirmations. Studies reveal that it takes four positive comments to counteract a single negative one. No wonder babies are so happy—constant positive affirmations surround them. Parents and families shower them with sweet, playful comments day in and day out: "You're so cute. Look at those chubby cheeks. You're so adorable. I love you so much!" The ratio of positive to negative comments for babies is almost 99% to 1% (with the 1% reserved for those late-night crying sessions).

As we age, that ratio shifts drastically. The stream of affirmations slows, and we hear far more criticism and negativity. Over time, this change doesn't just affect us individually; it trickles into our relationships. If you want a relationship where your partner feels empowered, trusted, and appreciated, you need to express it—frequently. Tell them. Show them. Don't assume they already know how you feel simply because they're around you or because you think they can read your mind.

Here's the truth: most people don't possess the ability to read minds. They might sense your feelings, but assumptions aren't enough to foster a real connection. For someone to honestly know how you feel, **actions and words must work together.** One without the other is like giving a baby a bottle without any milk—it looks like care on the outside, but it leaves the other person unfulfilled.

Simple Words, Big Impact

Building a relationship filled with positivity requires intentionality. Celebrate your partner with affirmations that build them up, just like you would a child learning to navigate the world. A kind word, or even a simple "I appreciate you," has the power to strengthen your connection and remind your partner of their value.

Compliments, compliments, compliments. Who doesn't love hearing a genuine compliment? It's often said that food is the way to a man's heart. If that's true, compliments are a direct highway to making a woman smile and feel secure. Don't believe me? The next time you see your partner, try saying, "That shirt looks really nice on you." If compliments haven't been a regular part of your conversations, she might initially be a little surprised or caught off guard. But I guarantee she'll be smiling on the inside.

It's crucial to verbalize the things we notice and appreciate. Think of it like a child who brings home straight A's for the fourth year in a row. Even if you've told them every other year that they're doing a fantastic job, it's still essential to keep acknowledging their effort. Why? Because, as humans, we all have an inherent need to feel seen and valued. Compliments are one of the simplest ways to meet that need, both in children and in relationships.

Consider this: if you received a bonus every time you completed an assignment at work, wouldn't that motivate you to go the extra mile? Most people would agree. I know I would! It's always nice to know that your hard work and effort aren't going unnoticed. The same principle applies to your partner. Compliments, even on the little things, reinforce that they are appreciated and loved.

For example, if she gets her nails done, she might be doing it purely for her own joy and confidence. But a quick "Your nails look great" from you can still brighten her day. It's a reminder that her efforts—no matter how big or small—don't go unnoticed by the person who matters most.

Compliments are a simple yet powerful tool for fostering connection and showing gratitude in your relationship. They require minimal effort but have a lasting impact. So don't hold back—acknowledge the things you admire and appreciate about your partner. Over time, these small affirmations will deepen your bond and bring more joy to both of your lives.

Navigating Tough Topics: Turning Conflict into Connection

One of the most challenging aspects of communication is delivering information that someone may not want to hear. These conversations often come with uncertainty about how the message will be received or how it will make the other person feel. I strive to avoid making anyone feel bad or upset—unless, of course, they're a Cowboys fan. But jokes aside, the real question is: how can we communicate difficult truths without causing unnecessary sadness or anger?

The answer lies in carefully "wrapping" our message in compassion—much like the bubble wrap used to protect fragile items during shipping. When you receive something delicate in the mail, it's typically encased in bubble wrap. This protective layer absorbs potential damage, ensuring the item arrives intact and retains its value. Similarly, when engaging in challenging conversations, we must cushion our words to preserve the relationship's integrity while still addressing the issue at hand.

Tough conversations should always begin with a positive statement. Think of this as the top layer of bubble wrap. Starting with something kind or affirming sets the tone for the discussion and reminds both parties that the conversation is grounded in good intentions. Once the foundation is laid, you can then transition to the issue at hand, framing it as *your perspective* rather than an accusation. This subtle shift helps prevent defensiveness and keeps the focus on collaboration rather than confrontation. Finally, as the conversation concludes, it's important to end on a positive note, which acts as the bottom layer of bubble wrap. This ensures that the last impression of the discussion is one of care and mutual respect.

WRAP YOUR WORDS LIKE THEY'RE FRAGILE.

You may be wondering about the "sides" of the bubble wrap. These are the moments within the conversation where you express care and reaffirm the relationship. By weaving in statements that emphasize your support or affection, you create a steady reminder that you are on the same team.

This approach not only softens the impact of difficult truths but also strengthens the relationship by fostering trust and understanding.

While the concept may seem simple, it's highly effective. Ending a challenging conversation on a positive note leaves a lasting memory of encouragement and collaboration. Wrapping your message in love and compassion ensures that both the content and the connection remain intact. Just like bubble wrap protects fragile items, this thoughtful approach safeguards the value of your relationships, even when discussing complex topics.

Here's how this method might look in action when addressing a lighthearted yet bothersome issue, like your partner chewing loudly:

Him: "You know, one of the things I really love about us is how much fun we have during meals together. It's honestly one of those little moments I look forward to—it makes our time so special."

Her: (smiling) "Aw, that's sweet! I love that, too. Dinner with you is always the best part of my day."

Him: "I've noticed something recently, and it's kind of silly, but I wanted to share it with you. Sometimes, when we're eating, the way you chew catches my attention. It's one of those small things that distracts me a little, and I know it's not intentional, but I thought it was worth mentioning because I value how much I enjoy our meals together."

Her: (raising an eyebrow) "Wait, are you saying I chew too loudly? I didn't even realize that was a thing!"

Him: (laughing lightly) "No, no, it's not that dramatic—it's just something I've picked up on. And honestly, it's more about me than you. I think I might just be overly sensitive to sounds sometimes. I didn't want to make it a big deal, but I figured we could talk about it."

Her: "Okay, that's fair. I mean, I can see how that might be annoying. Thanks for telling me in such a nice way."

Him: "I hope this doesn't come across the wrong way because I absolutely love the time we spend eating and talking together. I don't want to let something as small as chewing distract me from how much I enjoy being with you."

Her: (smiling warmly) "I get it. And I appreciate you being honest about it. I'll try to be more mindful of it, but feel free to let me know if I'm doing it again."

Him: "Thanks, that means a lot. I'm so grateful we can talk about even the small things like this. It makes me feel closer to you, and I love that we're able to share and grow together."

Her: "Me too. It's nice that we can laugh about this kind of stuff while still working through it. I feel the same way!"

This conversational format highlights the use of positivity, perspective, and reinforcement throughout, making the discussion productive, respectful, and even a little lighthearted.

By layering the conversation with positivity, perspective, and reassurance, the message becomes easier to digest. Even if the topic is uncomfortable, this method minimizes defensiveness and ensures the relationship remains strong. Difficult conversations don't have to be destructive—they can actually strengthen bonds when approached with care. Bubble-wrapping your words may take a little extra time and effort, but it's an investment in your relationship's longevity and trust.

Bible Time

Who: Elijah
What: God speaks through a whisper, not chaos
Where: 1 Kings 19:11–12

The Creator of all is undoubtedly the best communicator of all. One of the most profound examples of God's approach to communication is found in the story of the prophet Elijah. Elijah, fearful for his life, fled to Mount Horeb and sought refuge in a cave. As he waited for the Lord, he experienced a series of dramatic natural events: an earthquake, a mighty wind, and a consuming fire. Yet, the all-powerful God did not choose to reveal Himself through these overwhelming displays of force. Instead, the Lord came to Elijah in a whisper—a "still small voice."

As the Scripture recounts in **1 Kings 19:11-12 (KJV):**
"And he said, Go forth, and stand upon the mount before the Lord. And, behold, the Lord passed by, and a great and strong wind rent the mountains, and brake in pieces the rocks before the Lord; but the Lord was not in the wind: and after the wind an earthquake; but the Lord was not in the earthquake: and after the earthquake a fire; but the Lord was not in the fire: and after the fire a still small voice."

It was after hearing this gentle whisper that Elijah was able to step out of the cave and continue the work God had prepared for him. This moment teaches us a valuable lesson about the power of quiet, intentional communication. Sometimes we think that speaking louder or responding more forcefully will make others hear us or understand our point. Yet, the most omnipotent being in existence chose a calm, measured response in the midst of chaos. This example shows us how we, too, should respond in challenging situations, especially within the context of our relationships.

The Bible repeatedly emphasizes the profound impact our words can have. Communication is not only about conveying a message but also about how that message is delivered. Words have the power to build or destroy, to heal or to harm. When spoken with care and love, they can bring peace and clarity, even in the midst of tension. Consider these verses:

- **Proverbs 15:1 (KJV):**
  "A soft answer turneth away wrath: but grievous words stir up anger."

- **Proverbs 18:21 (KJV):**
  "Death and life are in the power of the tongue: and they that love it shall eat the fruit thereof."

Elijah's experience and these biblical principles underscore the importance of thoughtful, calm communication in our relationships. Whether addressing a conflict with a partner, guiding a child, or navigating difficult situations at work, the way we speak can make all the difference. Just as God chose a whisper to inspire action in Elijah, we too can use soft, intentional words to bring resolution and understanding.

When we choose calmness over chaos, we reflect the character of God in our communication, fostering peace and building stronger, healthier relationships.

LISTENING ON PURPOSE

WHERE WORDS MEET UNDERSTANDING

"Let every man be swift to hear, slow to speak, slow to wrath."

Have you ever seen a mother with her infant, and the baby starts crying? Then you hear the mother confidently say, "The baby is hungry." How could she possibly know what the baby needs just by the sound of the cry? Does she have superpowers that let her read the baby's mind? Some might say yes!

Interestingly, a study conducted by the Indiana University School of Medicine found that men typically use one hemisphere of their brain to listen, while women use both. Fellas, if you've ever struggled to listen, there's your scientific justification. Just kidding! The reality is that we all have two ears and one mouth, which suggests we should listen twice as much as we talk.

If you're in a relationship—or want to be—and you're looking to take things to the next level, listening will be the key. Imagine if you could always understand precisely what your partner wanted or needed every time she spoke. Do you think that would make her happy? The truth is, most women will tell you *exactly* what they want about 90% of the time. However, the challenge isn't whether men are listening—it's whether they're interpreting correctly.

It may sound strange, but even though men and women might speak the same language, their communication styles can be drastically different. Men tend to be direct, while women often express themselves in a more nuanced, roundabout way. For instance, your girlfriend might ask you, "Do you think she's pretty?" Fellas, let me save you some trouble: she does *not* actually want to know if you think someone else is attractive. What she's really asking is for reassurance—she wants to hear how beautiful you think *she* is. It's an opportunity for you to make her feel like the most important and gorgeous woman in your world. Questions like these often stem from insecurities, and your response can help build her confidence and strengthen your bond.

It may seem counterintuitive at first, but learning to listen beyond the words is one of the most powerful ways to connect. Women often communicate in layers, and listening with intention—not just hearing—will help you decode what they truly mean. Effective communication isn't just about words; it's about understanding, empathy, and showing that you value what your partner has to say.

Body Language

Pay close attention to facial expressions and body language—they often reveal what words do not. Just as with babies, subtle cues can be a clear giveaway of how someone is feeling. For example, when a baby is tired, they'll often rub their eyes, signaling their need for rest. Similarly, a lack of eye contact from your partner is usually a strong indicator that something is amiss. When your partner avoids looking at you or her eyes are downcast, it may suggest she's upset or processing emotions. Eye contact is a way to connect, and when it's withheld, it often reflects unresolved feelings or an unwillingness to engage emotionally in that moment. Think of this as an emotional wound that needs tending. Your ears become the bandage for her emotional pain, and this is your opportunity to help stop the "bleeding."

Begin with care and empathy, using a gentle approach like: *"It seems like something might be on your mind—do you want to talk about it?"* If she isn't receptive, try fostering a sense of closeness through nonverbal cues, such as sitting beside her or holding her hand. While this won't guarantee an immediate response, it demonstrates that you're present, attentive, and interested in supporting her. Without pressuring her to open up, reassure her by saying: *"You don't have to talk if you're not ready, but I just want you to know I'm here for you."* This keeps the door open for her to revisit the conversation when she feels ready while also showing that you respect her boundaries.

Sometimes, despite knowing something is off, your partner might not be ready to talk, creating a sense of awkwardness. To ease the tension, suggest a light activity to help both of you shift focus: *"Want to watch a movie or go for a walk and get some fresh air?"* Over time, this process fosters a sense of safety and emotional trust. Your partner will feel seen, supported, and more willing to open up in the future.

Furthermore, while eye contact is a significant clue, it's just one piece of the puzzle. Your partner may communicate that something is wrong through other nonverbal cues, such as their posture—like sitting with crossed arms—or their tone of voice. Each person has unique signals, so your role is to notice what's different from their usual behavior.

For instance, imagine your partner usually is very bubbly and talkative in the evenings, sharing stories about their day or asking about yours. One evening, however, they come home, say a quick hello, and retreat to the couch without much conversation. When you ask about their day, they give short, vague answers like "It was fine" or "Same as usual," and they avoid making eye contact. This shift in behavior might seem minor, but it could be a sign that something is weighing on their mind. Another example could be a change in physical affection. Let's say your partner usually gives you a hug and kiss every morning before you leave for work. One morning, they're distant, barely looking up from their coffee as you say goodbye. This small change could indicate they're upset, preoccupied, or even feeling unappreciated.

When you notice these changes, it's time to channel your inner detective and thoughtfully approach the situation. Responding with care and sensitivity is essential, as you won't fully understand what's going on until they're ready to share it with you.

Scroll, Listen, Engage

The same way social media can elevate your communication with your partner, it can also enhance your listening skills—if you pay attention. Social media often serves as an outlet for expressing emotions, even when it might not seem like the healthiest way to do so. While I'm not here to debate the appropriateness of airing personal concerns online, it's undeniable that people, including your partner, often use social media to convey feelings they may struggle to express directly.

For instance, your partner might post videos or share memes about men not helping around the house or spending too much time on video games. If her first instinct is to go to social media instead of discussing the issue with you, it's natural to feel frustrated. However, in the middle of such a situation, focusing on that frustration—like critiquing the "paint job on a ship during a storm"—is counterproductive. The real goal is to navigate the storm itself. Only after things settle should you address how to weather future storms more effectively.

With that in mind, pay attention. Sometimes your partner might not have the words to articulate their feelings directly but may use a video, a meme, or a story post to convey emotions. Be open to seeing and hearing what they're trying to communicate, even if it's through an unconventional medium. It's not always about how the message is delivered but what the message truly is.

Consider the saying, "It's not what you say, but how you say it." While tone and delivery do matter, the actual message carries the most weight. For example, if your child is about to touch a hot stove, you wouldn't calmly and gently say, "Please don't touch the stove." The urgency and clarity of the message outweigh the tone at that moment. Similarly, in your relationship, the content of your partner's message is what deserves the most attention. How it was delivered can be addressed later—but understanding what's being communicated should always come first.

For example, if your partner is feeling self-conscious about aging or not feeling as attractive as they once did, they might share videos or posts about how men should compliment their wives and make them feel special. Ideally, they'd communicate those feelings directly, but maybe they don't know how. This is where you need to step in—not to criticize how they've chosen to express themselves but to show that you're listening and create a space where they feel safe enough to share openly in the future.

> **Being an elite listener means look-**
> **ing past the surface—whether**
> **that's tone, delivery, or plat-**
> **form—and focusing on the heart of**
> **the message.**

When you acknowledge and address your partner's emotions with care and understanding, you strengthen the foundation of your relationship and make it easier for both of you to communicate more effectively moving forward.

Listening vs Hearing

Many people assume that hearing and listening are the same, but they are fundamentally different. Hearing is a physiological process—your ears pick up sound waves and send them to your brain. It's passive and automatic, something that happens without conscious effort. Listening, on the other hand, is an active skill. It requires focus, attention, and the intent to understand not just the words but the meaning and emotions behind them. Imagine sitting in a busy coffee shop. You can hear the clatter of cups, the hum of conversations, and the hiss of the espresso machine. But unless you consciously tune in to the conversation at your table, you're not truly listening to the person in front of you. Listening demands engagement—it's not enough to let words wash over you; you need to process and respond in a way that shows you care.

This distinction becomes even more pronounced in everyday relationships. Consider a parent with their child. A child may say, "I don't want to go to school," but the tone of their voice or the sadness in their eyes may tell a deeper story. If the parent is merely hearing, they might respond with, "You have to go to school—it's not up for debate." But if the parent is listening, they might recognize the reluctance as anxiety, frustration, or even bullying. By asking questions like, "What's making you feel this way?" or "Is something bothering you at school?" the parent demonstrates empathy and creates an opportunity for a deeper connection. The same principle applies to romantic relationships. Imagine your partner asking, "Does this outfit look okay?" If you're only hearing, you might respond with a quick "Yes, it looks fine" without thinking twice. However, listening goes beyond the surface and recognizes the underlying need for reassurance. Maybe there's hesitation in her tone or a hint of self-consciousness in her posture. A thoughtful listener would respond with something more meaningful, like, "You look amazing—I love how that color brings out your eyes." This kind of response not only addresses the question but also reinforces her confidence and shows that you truly see her.

Whether it's your child recounting their day at school or your partner expressing frustration about something, intentional listening means putting your phone down, maintaining eye contact, and giving cues—like nodding or paraphrasing—to show you're engaged. This intentionality creates a sense of safety and trust, making the other person feel valued and heard. True listening also involves thoughtful responses and follow-up. When your child confides in you about a challenging situation, take the time to ask clarifying questions or suggest ways to help. When your partner opens up about her feelings, reflect back what you've heard and offer support. Avoid the temptation to fix the problem immediately—sometimes, the act of listening is all they need. Now, men, I know this part can be challenging.

SOMETIMES, THE SOLUTION IS JUST LISTEN-ING.

Our thought processes often lean toward being linear and solution-oriented, and we're quick to want to fix things. But sometimes, the solution *is* listening. There are moments when your partner doesn't need answers; she needs to vent and release her emotions. Recognizing these moments is a critical part of emotional intelligence. It's about understanding that the response you might want in the same situation isn't always what someone else needs. Listening with this awareness can strengthen your connection and show that you genuinely understand and care.

From Listening to Feeling

Now, it's time to truly connect on an emotional level. Women often tap into a wide range of emotions, and it's crucial, as a listener, to empathize with the feelings being expressed or exhibited. It's easy to lose sight of your partner's emotions, especially during an argument or when you hold a different perspective on what's happened. However, when you're in the role of the listener, your feelings take a backseat. Your primary focus should be using both your ears and your heart to understand what your partner is experiencing emotionally.

Let me break this down with an example. Suppose your partner says she feels like you don't care about her and that you're neglecting your relationship because you chose to watch a Lakers game instead of the "Love is Blind" finale. Now, you might feel this is unfair—you've only watched one game in the last 30 days, and you believe you spend most of your free time with her. But this moment isn't about defending yourself or proving her wrong. It's about hearing and validating her feelings.

First and foremost, address the emotions being expressed. Whether or not you agree with her perception, the fact remains that she feels uncared for. If you genuinely care about your partner, you don't want her to feel this way. Acknowledge her emotions by saying something like, *"I'm so sorry you feel like I don't care about you. I love you and absolutely care about you."*

This simple step allows you both to find common ground, even in the midst of a disagreement. By validating her feelings, you help her feel heard, important, and valued. That emotional connection is the foundation for resolving the underlying issue.

Once you've validated her emotions, the next step is to work toward understanding and resolution. Ask clarifying questions to ensure you comprehend her perspective fully. For instance, you might say, *"Can you tell me more about what made you feel this way? I want to understand better."* This keeps the conversation open and demonstrates your genuine interest in her feelings. From there, look for ways to bridge the gap. Perhaps you can agree to set aside a specific night for her favorite show or find a balance that works for both of you. The goal is to not only resolve the current issue but also to create a dynamic where your partner feels heard and supported in the future. When you consistently approach disagreements with empathy and validation, you strengthen the bond between you and your partner, fostering trust and emotional intimacy. Listening on an emotional level is a skill, but with practice, it will become a powerful tool in deepening your relationship.

Empathetic listening allows you to truly connect with your partner, sometimes even to the point of sharing in their emotions. There may be moments when they need you to cry with them or meet them exactly where they are emotionally. As the Bible says, *"Rejoice with those who rejoice; mourn with those who mourn."* Connecting on as many emotional levels as possible is vital in a relationship. When your partner trusts you enough to share their deepest emotions—ones they might not reveal to anyone else—welcome those moments with compassion and open arms. Be their safe space, a refuge where they feel seen, heard, and understood. Everyone needs that kind of support.

Jesus' example of deep, compassionate listening offers a powerful model for all of us. Throughout His ministry, He didn't just hear the words of those around Him—He listened with His heart. He recognized their pain, fears, and needs, and He responded with love and truth. Whether it was the woman at the well, Zacchaeus in the tree, or the disciples struggling to understand His teachings, He showed that listening is an act of grace and connection. When we listen with empathy and intention, we build relationships rooted in care, understanding, and trust. Let us strive to listen not just with our ears but with our hearts, embracing the profound impact of truly hearing others.

"Rejoice with them that do rejoice, and weep with them that weep."

Story Time

An emphasis on listening is crucial to a successful relationship. One of my good friends and his spouse are a great example of how listening with intention can have life-altering effects. Their story, which Anthony relayed to me, illustrates the transformative power of truly hearing and acting on a partner's needs.

Maya sat on the couch, scrolling through old family photos, her expression distant. Anthony noticed and asked, "What's on your mind?"

Maya hesitated before admitting, "I miss my family. It feels like I never see them anymore. Life just keeps getting in the way."

Anthony paused, taking in her words. "I get it. Family is so important to you. That must be really hard," he said. Maya softened, grateful for his understanding.

Over the next week, Anthony took action. He checked their calendar and suggested a weekend trip to visit her family, followed by inviting them over to stay. He even worked with her sister to set up regular video calls.

When Maya realized what Anthony had done, she was overwhelmed. "You really listened," she told him. "It means so much to me."

Anthony smiled. "It matters to you, so it matters to me. I want you to feel connected to the people you love."

From that point forward, the effort to prioritize Maya's family became a part of their life. Whether it was a road trip, hosting her family at their home, or simply scheduling time to chat, Anthony's commitment to listening and acting on Maya's needs deepened their bond. This story demonstrates the power of intentional listening. It's not just about hearing words—it's about understanding the heart behind them and responding in a way that makes your partner feel valued and supported. For Maya, it wasn't just about seeing her family more often—it was about feeling heard and loved by the person she shared her life with.

When we listen with intention and empathy, we strengthen our relationships and create a foundation of trust and mutual care. Sometimes, the simple act of listening can lead to profound changes, not just in the moment but in the overall connection we share with the people we love.

THE 4 PS

PRAYER, PATIENCE, PRACTICE, AND PERSISTENCE

T he **4 Ps—Prayer, Patience, Practice, and Persistence** are the foundational pillars of building and maintaining strong, meaningful relationships. Whether navigating the complexities of parenting, the daily challenges of marriage, or even our spiritual walk with God, these principles provide a roadmap for responding to frustrations and cultivating love and understanding. Rooted in biblical wisdom, the 4 Ps equip us to approach recurring difficulties with grace, aligning our hearts with God's purpose while actively working toward resolution.

These principles not only transform how we handle conflicts but also deepen our connection with others, mirroring the way Christ faithfully nurtures His relationship with the Church. Through prayer, we invite God's guidance; through patience, we endure with love; through practice, we take deliberate action; and through persistence, we stay committed even when progress seems slow. Together, the 4 Ps empower us to face life's relational challenges with faith and resilience.

Prayer: Pause with God

Prayer is a powerful tool for cultivating patience in any relationship. When challenges arise, prayer serves as a lifeline, offering guidance, strength, and peace. Both parents and spouses can use prayer to seek divine wisdom and perspective, transforming moments of frustration into opportunities for growth. Whether a parent is overwhelmed by a child's disobedience or a husband struggles with his wife's recurring habits, prayer aligns the heart with God's love, enabling a more compassionate response.

Imagine a parent dealing with a child who consistently refuses to do homework. Despite multiple attempts to enforce rules and set expectations, the child remains resistant. In such moments, frustration can easily take over, leading to harsh words or strained interactions. However, by pausing to pray, the parent invites God into the situation, asking for wisdom and patience. This allows for an opportunity to re-group and re-focus and let whatever issue has occurred be brought down to its normal size. Oftentimes, in the midst of a difficult situation, we struggle with the feeling of being overwhelmed, and every detail seems magnified. Prayer not only calms the parent's heart but also opens the door for God to work in the child's life. **James 1:5** reminds us, "If any of you lacks wisdom, you should ask God, who gives generously to all without finding fault, and it will be given to you."

Similarly, in marriage, prayer can transform how a husband responds to his wife's actions. For instance, if his wife repeatedly leaves dishes in the sink, rather than immediately reacting with irritation, he can turn to prayer. This act of seeking God's help allows him to process his emotions and respond with grace rather than frustration. The time to submit to something greater than oneself will enable us to put events in their rightful pecking order. For example, if you're married, there should be enough love equity built up so that when you're going through a tough time, you can lean on that equity. In the previous example, if you see the dishes left in the sink, ask yourself these questions: Does my spouse (or future spouse) love me? Does my partner have my best interest at heart? Does my partner want to want to annoy or irritate me intentionally? If the answer to the 1st two questions is yes, then I can assure you the last answer is no. They do not want to annoy or irritate you intentionally. It may *feel* like it, but a part of emotional intelligence leads you to understand that how you think about a situation isn't always indicative of the other person's intentions. Oftentimes, our feelings will blind us from the reality of the situation. So, as an alternative to being irritated, start to look at what may be a roadblock to your partner completing what you've expected. Do they even know you expect the dishes to be cleaned? We assume our partners are mind readers and should know everything about us. However, it takes a lifetime to know just a portion of a person. Do you know what they might be dealing with internally? Maybe, they had a really rough workday and need to decompress. Or they might feel overwhelmed by the difficulties and expectations of life. That is why prayer is a great starting place. Prayer often changes not only the situation but also the heart of the one praying, shifting the focus from the problem to God's capacity to work through it.

"Prayer often changes not just the situation—but the heart of the one praying."

Jesus modeled the power of prayer in His relationship with the Church. Before His crucifixion, He prayed for His disciples, asking God to protect and unify them. In **John 17:20-21**, He prayed not only for His immediate followers but also for all who would believe in Him through their message. This example of intercession demonstrates that prayer is not just about asking for solutions but also about seeking alignment with God's will and purpose. Through prayer, parents and spouses can cultivate the patience needed to navigate recurring challenges. Prayer provides the strength to endure, the wisdom to guide, and the love to respond with grace. It reminds us that we are not alone in our struggles and that God's presence is ever ready to sustain us.

Patience: Wait with Grace

Most people will say they have patience but do not know what the word actually means. According to the Cambridge Dictionary, patience is:

> the ability to wait, or to continue doing something despite difficulties, or to **suffer without complaining or becoming annoyed.**

Sometimes, individuals feel that because they've waited for a while, they have exhibited patience. Unfortunately, that's only half the battle. In the midst of waiting, we must do so gracefully without complaining or becoming annoyed. It sounds daunting, but it's extremely rewarding. To foster healthy relationships, particularly those between parents and children, and husbands and wives, patience is a foundational pillar. These dynamics are filled with recurring challenges that test the limits of our understanding, love, and endurance. Just as a father or mother must display patience in teaching their child the same lesson repeatedly, a husband must also exhibit patience when dealing with habits or actions from his wife that may irritate him. In both relationships, patience is not only a virtue but a deliberate choice rooted in love and a commitment to foster growth.

PATIENCE ISN'T JUST WAITING—IT'S HOW YOU WAIT.

Consider the common example of a parent teaching their newborn to talk. For the 1st year of that child's life, the parents will say thousands of words to them, mostly "Ma Ma" and "Da Da," hoping the child will imitate their words with little success. However, most parents do not get frustrated or irritated with their children because they recognize that talking takes time and is a process. I believe in the *hope* of the eventual day when their little one will say their first words. There's something in the midst of the waiting to focus on instead of complaining. Also, progress is recognized and celebrated. For example, if their child says gibberish or what many would call "Baby Talk," the parents celebrate and say "Good Job" to reinforce the good behavior in hopes that it will be repeated and progress. These steps are essential to the growth of the child. Similarly, in a marital relationship, a husband might find himself frustrated by his wife's lack of physical intimacy. The initial thought may be to get irritated and frustrated, but how does that help you, your partner, or the problem? Most of the time, complaining about the problem may decrease the likelihood of you getting the expected outcome. Alternatively, reinforcing the progress your partner is currently making. Something as simple as your partner holding your hand, you can emphasize how grateful you are and how it makes you feel connected. This will remind your partner that intimacy matters to you. You can communicate what you need or want but with love instead of complaints. Then, the difficult part is waiting. In today's society, we're accustomed to immediate gratification, but human habits have their own timelines. Changes occur over time, so any issue you may have with your partner will not be resolved overnight. Hold on to the hope of the day when things will be resolved, but acknowledge the progress along the way. You'd be surprised how far saying, "I can see the effort you've been putting in, and I really appreciate it. It means a lot to me," can go for someone. It helps your partner feel seen, fostering an inner sense of hope for a better tomorrow while embracing the belief that today is an improvement over yesterday.

Furthermore, the Bible emphasizes patience as essential for growth and relationships. In **Proverbs 22:6**, we are instructed to "Train up a child in the way he should go: and when he is old, he will not depart from it." This guidance acknowledges that training a child is a process requiring repeated effort and perseverance. Similarly, in marriage, patience fosters growth and harmony over time. Relationships are not static; they require consistent effort and grace to thrive. Christ's relationship with the Church exemplifies the ultimate model of patience. In **2 Peter 3:9**, we are reminded that "The Lord is not slow in keeping his promise, as some understand slowness. Instead, he is patient with you, not wanting anyone to perish, but everyone to come to repentance." Just as Christ patiently waits for the Church to mature in faith, parents and spouses are called to extend patience to their loved ones. The journey of growth—whether in a child learning responsibility or a spouse adapting to shared expectations—takes time and understanding.

Ultimately, patience in both relationships reflects Christ's love. By choosing patience over frustration, parents and spouses create environments where growth can flourish. These relationships become spaces of grace, much like Christ's relationship with His Church, where imperfections are met with love, and progress is celebrated over perfection.

Practice: Act with Intention

Patience is not just an attitude, but a skill that requires deliberate practice. Both parents and spouses must actively work on cultivating patience in their daily interactions. By responding thoughtfully to frustrating situations, they reinforce their commitment to growth and demonstrate love in action. This practice involves intentionality, choosing to act with kindness even when emotions suggest otherwise.

For parents, practice often means finding creative ways to address recurring issues. For example, if a child struggles to remember to put away their toys, a parent might create a chart with rewards for consistent effort. This system teaches the child responsibility while also training the parent in patience through repetition and reinforcement. Similarly, in marriage, a husband might choose to approach his wife's habits with understanding and proactive solutions. If the dishes remain undone, he might wash them himself as an act of love or have a calm conversation about shared responsibilities.

Jesus provides a perfect example of practicing patience in relationships. In **Mark 9:33-37**, when His disciples argued about who was the greatest, Jesus did not rebuke them harshly. Instead, He gently corrected their perspective, using the moment as an opportunity to teach humility and service. This approach required patience and a willingness to address the issue constructively rather than reactively. Parents and spouses can learn from this example by viewing frustrating situations as opportunities to build connection and understanding.

Practicing patience is not easy, especially when the same issues arise repeatedly. However, each instance is an opportunity to grow in love and grace. By choosing to respond with patience, both parents and spouses build stronger, more resilient relationships, mirroring the love Christ shows to His Church.

Persistence: Stay with Love

Persistence transforms fleeting patience into a lasting, transformative force. In both parenting and marriage, persistence ensures that love remains steadfast despite repeated challenges. Whether it's teaching a child a new habit or addressing recurring frustrations with a spouse, persistence allows relationships to grow and thrive.

A father teaching his child to ride a bike may face moments of hesitation or falls, yet his steady encouragement and support gradually build the child's confidence and skill. Similarly, a husband navigating his wife's habits benefits from showing patience and understanding. For example, if his wife frequently forgets to pay a bill, he might gently remind her, suggest setting up automated payments, or even take on the responsibility himself. Such persistence, though at times challenging, becomes a powerful expression of love and commitment, reflecting the depth of his care in the face of frustration.

Now, you may be thinking that some things are too important to mess up. Well, everyone makes mistakes, big and small. Navigating through life, we must extend the same grace that we hope to receive. As partners, we should actively seek opportunities to make our loved one's world a little easier. Relationships are not about keeping score or assigning blame but about teamwork and mutual growth. If a student struggles to learn how to read, is that truly the fault of the student or a reflection of the teaching approach? Too often, we rush to criticize the person who is struggling instead of stepping back to evaluate how we might help in a more effective or compassionate way.

RELATIONSHIPS AREN'T A SCORE-BOARD—THEY'RE A GRACE GAME.

Just as a dedicated teacher exhausts every method and approach to reach their student, partners in a relationship should embrace the same mindset—adapting, understanding, and finding new ways to connect and support. This effort requires humility, empathy, and a willingness to see challenges not as obstacles but as opportunities to deepen the bond. Ultimately, offering grace and understanding not only eases the weight of mistakes but also strengthens the foundation of trust and love, fostering a partnership where both people can thrive. The Bible emphasizes persistence as a key aspect of patience. In **Galatians 6:9**, Paul advises, "Let us not become weary in doing good, for at the proper time we will reap a harvest if we do not give up." This encouragement reminds us that persistence often leads to long-term growth and blessings, even when immediate results are not visible. Christ's persistence with the Church serves as the ultimate model. Despite humanity's repeated failures and shortcomings, Christ's love never wavers. He continues to intercede for His followers, as seen in **Hebrews 7:25**, where it states that He "always lives to intercede for them." This relentless commitment calls parents and spouses to persist in their roles, trusting that their efforts will bear fruit over time.

By combining prayer, practice, patience, and persistence, we can navigate the recurring challenges of relationships with grace and wisdom. These "4 P's" not only strengthen our connections with loved ones but also reflect the love Christ has for His Church—a love that is patient, persistent, and transformative.

Story Time

The concept of the 4 Ps may sound great in theory, but do they truly work in practice? Consider the example of Timothy and Lisa, a married couple with contrasting personalities and approaches to life. Timothy, with his analytical background, is highly organized and detail-oriented, while Lisa is creative, expressive, and more spontaneous. Their differences began to create tension at home. Timothy often felt frustrated, perceiving Lisa as less productive when it came to household chores, as she frequently became absorbed in creative projects or seized the moment to pursue other interests. The result was an unorganized home, which heightened Timothy's stress. However, instead of allowing his frustration to boil over, Timothy decided to take a different approach. He prayed for guidance and sought direction.

To his surprise, he felt inspired to create lists to help organize the household tasks—a concept foreign to Timothy, as he naturally kept things in order mentally. Despite his reservations, he shared the idea with Lisa, who was surprisingly receptive. Lisa explained that she often used lists at work to stay organized and on task, so the suggestion felt familiar and manageable. The first week of implementing this new system was a bit clunky as they both adjusted to the process. However, over time, it became a game-changer. Within a month, their home was far more organized, and Lisa felt a newfound sense of peace. Knowing exactly what needed to be done each day helped her feel less overwhelmed and more accomplished by the end of each week.

For Timothy, the transformation was equally satisfying. The home was finally in order, and he had successfully addressed the issue without burdening or alienating his wife. Instead, he had supported her in a way that aligned with her strengths and needs. This experience exemplified how intentional communication, thoughtful action, and mutual understanding can bridge gaps in relationships and create a more harmonious partnership. He didn't just fix the mess—he fortified the marriage.

SACRIFICE: THE SOIL OF BLESSINGS

THE HEARTWORK OF LOVING WITHOUT LIMITS

"And let us not be weary in well doing: for in due season we shall reap, if we faint not."

Sacrifice—a word that carries immense weight and meaning. Almost everyone can recall a moment when they sacrificed for someone else or benefited from the sacrifices of others, especially parents. I can attest to the unwavering generosity of my parents, who would have given me the shirt off their backs to ensure I had a better life. Too often, parents take on jobs they don't love, lose sleep, and set aside their dreams, all for the well-being of their children. Why? Because of an unbreakable, innate love and a deep sense of responsibility to provide. This selfless love and willingness to sacrifice are essential in nurturing a fulfilling relationship with a significant other, fostering connection, growth, and mutual respect.

Reframing Sacrifice: A Blessing, Not a Loss

The word "sacrifice" often carries a negative connotation, evoking the idea of losing something. But what if we viewed it differently? What if sacrifice, in itself, is a blessing? Consider this: having the capacity to give something up is a sign of strength. Take, for instance, individuals in rehabilitation facilities who face various addictions. Every time someone overcomes an addiction or lets go of something that holds them back, they are rewarded—not just with tangible tokens like a sobriety coin for an alcoholic who has remained sober for 24 hours—but also with intangible benefits such as peace of mind, self-respect, or the satisfaction of growth.

SACRIFICE ISN'T LOSS—IT'S PLANTING.

Sacrifice also creates space for something new to flourish. When we give up something lesser, it often makes way for something greater to enter our lives. Think about the farmer who sacrifices seeds by planting them in the soil. Initially, it may seem like a loss—those seeds are no longer visible or available—but in time, they yield an abundant harvest. In relationships, our sacrifices are like planting seeds of love, trust, and commitment. These acts may require effort or discomfort in the moment, but the harvest they produce—stronger connections, deeper intimacy, and mutual respect—is immeasurable.

Additionally, sacrifice is a choice, and making that choice demonstrates love and purpose. When you willingly sacrifice time, comfort, or resources for someone else, it reinforces your own capacity for selflessness and deepens the value of the relationship. Instead of viewing it as a burden, think of it as a gift you're giving to yourself as much as to others. Sacrifice can strengthen your character, build resilience, and remind you of your priorities. Ultimately, it's an opportunity to align your actions with the values and relationships that matter most to you.

Choosing Love Over Convenience

In relationships, the principle is much the same. We often place undue value on things that, in the grand scheme, don't truly matter. Picture this: you come home, and your partner wants to spend quality time with you, but the Lakers game is about to start (as a passionate sports fan, I can relate—if this doesn't resonate, substitute it with something meaningful to you). While I may love sports, my partner is the one who loves me back. Choosing to set aside one evening to connect with her may seem small, but the impact it leaves is profound and lasting. In this context, sacrifice becomes an investment in the strength and depth of your relationship.

On the other hand, prioritizing the game over spending time with your partner can have unintended consequences. In this scenario, your partner may feel undervalued, unimportant, or lonely due to the lack of quality time together. It's essential to recognize the simple yet profound blessing in their desire to spend time with you. There are countless individuals who long for the connection and companionship of someone who genuinely wants to share moments with them.

The Ripple Effect of Small Sacrifices

Relationships thrive on intentionality, and choosing to prioritize your partner reinforces their significance in your life. By valuing the time you share, you're not just creating memories but also building trust and emotional intimacy. Sacrificing something as fleeting as a game to nurture your relationship demonstrates maturity and a commitment to its growth. It's these small, everyday choices that create the foundation for a relationship that stands the test of time.

SMALL SACRIFICES BUILD BIG TRUST.
It's not the size of the sacrifice—it's the consistency that builds intimacy.

I challenge you to think back to a time when you made a sacrifice for someone else. How did it make you feel afterward? I remember, as a child, during the holiday season, when my family donated toys to children who wouldn't be receiving gifts due to financial hardships. Watching their faces light up with joy and excitement as they opened their presents was heartwarming. It was a moment of pure happiness, but it also made me reflect. I felt a sense of guilt, realizing how fortunate I had always been to have gifts under the tree. That experience taught me gratitude and inspired me to do more for others.

Now, think about your relationships. Do you have the capacity to give more, to go above and beyond for someone you truly care about? Imagine how incredible it would feel to know someone else put their heart and effort into making you happy. That kind of love and commitment is a gift in itself—a daily reminder that you're valued. But here's the truth: to receive that kind of selfless love, you must embody it. You reap what you sow, and in relationships, sowing seeds of sacrifice and generosity yields a harvest of trust, connection, and fulfillment.

Christ's Example and the Call to Daily Sacrifice

So, how far do we go with this sacrifice thing? Great question! The greatest sacrifice that has ever existed has been Christ laying down his life for his friends. That's deep, right? Think to yourself: if you have kids or if you plan to have them in the future, would you die for your kids? Most people would say yes. They'd be willing to sacrifice EVERYTHING for their kids. So why wouldn't you do the same for the person you choose to go through life with? Fortunately, we're not tasked with actual death daily. However, figuratively, we should die to our selfish ways on a daily basis. This will enable us to identify our partner's exact needs and fulfill them without regret. When looking at the lengths parents will go for their kids, something such as skipping a basketball game or doing the dishes seems like a cakewalk.

I challenge you to write down 3-5 things that your partner or your heart tells you you can sacrifice for the betterment of your relationship. Then, I want you to identify why and how removing or reducing them would impact you. I've learned that things we can't give up, at least for a little while, are addictions.

1. I can sacrifice:
Why it matters to me:
How it might strengthen my relationship:

2. I can sacrifice:
Why it matters to me:
How it might strengthen my relationship:

3. I can sacrifice:
Why it matters to me:
How it might strengthen my relationship:

4. I can sacrifice:
Why it matters to me:
How it might strengthen my relationship:

5. I can sacrifice:
Why it matters to me:
How it might strengthen my relationship:

The Power and Purpose of Sacrificial Love

What's the real benefit of sacrificing in your relationship? It's about building emotional and relational equity with your partner. But let's clarify—this isn't a transactional exchange where you expect something in return. True sacrifice isn't about leverage; it's about love. Imagine your partner as a vessel that needs to be filled, not with water but with love, care, and kindness. Every act of sacrifice you make is like pouring into that vessel. Do you want her cup to be empty, leaving her drained and unfulfilled? Or do you want it to overflow, enabling her to thrive and shine in every area of her life?

The goal is to create an environment where her "cup runs over," where the love and care you've poured into her overflow into everything she does—whether she's at work, spending time with family, or sharing moments with you. When a person feels truly cared for, it shows. Think about how you feel after a full-body massage. The masseuse sacrifices their energy, skill, and focus to help you relax and release stress. Afterward, you're not just physically rejuvenated—you're mentally reset, free from the burdens that weighed you down. Imagine coming home from a long day to a hot meal waiting for you, a warm smile, and maybe even a foot rub. Wouldn't you feel seen, appreciated, and loved? If the answer is yes, consider how you can offer that same care to your partner in ways that resonate with her needs.

"We give sacrificially because God first gave sacrificially to us."

Sacrificial love is about being proactive—doing for your partner what you know will fill her heart and soul. It's about being the change you want to see in your relationship. Treating your partner with the same care and intentionality you hope to receive creates a cycle of mutual love and respect. This isn't just about making your partner happy; it's about the joy you'll feel knowing you're contributing to her well-being. A full "love tank" empowers her to be the best version of herself—the person you fell in love with. So, invest in her happiness selflessly and consistently. The rewards—stronger intimacy, deeper connection, and mutual fulfillment—are worth every bit of effort.

Bible Time

Who: Elijah and the widow
What: Sacrifice
Where: 1 Kings 17:8-24

Elijah, a prophet of God, was directed to go to Zarephath during a severe drought with the promise that he would meet a widow who would provide him with food and water. Obediently, Elijah followed God's instruction and met the widow, who revealed a heartbreaking reality: she had only enough food for herself and her son to eat one final meal before succumbing to starvation. Despite her dire circumstances, Elijah asked her to make a sacrifice—to feed him first. Imagine the courage and faith that must have taken!

Remarkably, the widow chose to do the uncomfortable and selfless thing. Her act of trust opened the door for God's blessing. In return, God performed a miracle: her flour jar and oil jug never ran out, and her household ate for many days, just as God had promised.

Later, the widow's son grew gravely ill, and she turned to Elijah for help. Elijah took the boy, cried out to God, and pleaded for the child's life. Moved by Elijah's faith, God responded, bringing the boy back to life.

This story illustrates the cyclical nature of sacrifice and blessing. In one season, the widow sacrificed to fill Elijah's cup. In another, Elijah's faith restored her child. Her initial act of trust sowed seeds that bore fruit when she needed it most. You never know how your sacrifice today might pave the way for blessings and restoration in the future.

CAN YOU ENDURE?

BUILDING LASTING LOVE THROUGH ADVERSITY

E ndurance is often overlooked as a critical trait in building and sustaining successful relationships. It is a quality that shines brightest in the context of parenthood, where the demands are relentless, but the love is unyielding.

Before I had children, I often spent time with my baby cousins. It was an enjoyable experience, full of laughter and affection. However, one of the perks of those moments was that I could always "give them back" at the end of the day. There was no long-term responsibility, no need to endure the challenges of sleepless nights or tantrums. Parenthood, on the other hand, is entirely different. Most parents do not want to give up on their children, no matter how difficult things get. There's an innate drive—an internal motor fueled by the "oil of love"—that keeps them going. This capacity to endure, day in and day out, is unmatched. Even on the most challenging days, parents find ways to persevere because their love provides a deep reservoir of strength.

Yet, when it comes to romantic relationships, endurance can sometimes feel elusive. Why is that? Why do relationships between partners often feel harder to sustain than the parent-child bond? The answer lies in the nature of effort and perspective. The emotional and physical energy required to maintain a romantic relationship can feel overwhelming at times. In those moments, it's easy to lose sight of what truly matters. The bond that brought you together may feel strained under the weight of daily stress, communication gaps, or unmet expectations.

But here's the good news: those feelings of exhaustion and frustration are entirely natural. Every relationship faces moments where endurance feels like a tall order. The key is not to deny or suppress these feelings but to address them with intention and strategy.

Safe Spaces

First and foremost, creating a safe space to communicate openly is essential for healthy relationships. This foundational step ensures misunderstandings are minimized, and issues that arise are addressed promptly rather than lingering and growing into larger problems. One of the biggest downfalls in relationships is what I call the **"gap period."** This is the time between when an issue arises and when it is resolved. The longer this period extends, the more opportunity there is for other variables—like frustration, resentment, or misinterpretation—to complicate the situation.

> **For example:** Imagine you and your partner have a date night planned for 7:30 PM. She takes three hours to get ready, making you late by an hour. You're frustrated and annoyed, but instead of expressing how you feel in the moment, you internalize your frustration and become distant during dinner. Your partner senses the shift in your energy and asks if something is wrong. Instead of addressing the issue, you brush it off and try to sweep it under the rug. Now, your partner feels frustrated because she perceives you as unwilling to

open up. Fast forward two days: the issue remains unresolved, and you're still holding onto your annoyance. Everything your partner does starts to irritate you, and the unresolved feelings ripple through your interactions. Eventually, you release your pent-up anger, but by this point, your partner feels blindsided and defensive. The original message is lost, and the conversation escalates into conflict.

Is this healthy? Absolutely not.

The gap period allows small problems to snowball into bigger ones. Instead of fostering understanding and resolution, it breeds resentment, miscommunication, and unnecessary tension. Think about how you handle issues with a child. For instance, if your child spills juice on the floor, you won't let the problem linger for days. You'd address it immediately, calmly explaining the situation and helping them clean it up. This ensures the issue is resolved, and there's no unnecessary build-up of frustration or miscommunication.

In relationships, the same principle applies: address problems promptly to prevent the "gap period" from creating emotional distance. Here's how:

1. **Acknowledge the Issue Early** If something bothers you, express it respectfully in the moment or shortly afterward. For example, if you're frustrated about being late for date night, you might say, "I feel a bit stressed because we're running behind, and I was really looking forward to getting there on time." This opens the door for discussion without assigning blame or letting resentment simmer.

2. **Choose Words Wisely** Just as you'd use gentle, constructive language with a child to foster learning rather than shame, approach your partner with care. Avoid accusations and absolute words like, "You **always** make us late," and instead focus on how the situation impacted you. For instance, "Being late made me feel anxious, and

I just want us to enjoy the evening together."

3. **Create a Safe, Open Space**. Ensure your partner feels comfortable expressing their perspective, too. A collaborative, solution-focused approach fosters understanding instead of defensiveness.

4. **Resolve and Move Forward** Once the issue is addressed, let it go—just as you would after helping a child clean up their spill. Holding onto the frustration will only magnify future conflicts.

With a child, your instinct is to resolve things quickly to teach them, maintain harmony, and prevent further issues. Applying this same mindset in your relationship not only avoids unnecessary tension but also demonstrates respect and commitment to nurturing the bond you share. By closing the gap early, you strengthen your partnership and prevent minor frustrations from growing into major conflicts.

Chop Wood Carry Water

One of the most impactful books I've read is *Chop Wood, Carry Water* by Joshua Medcalf. The core message of the book is simple yet profound: fall in love with the process, especially the seemingly mundane, routine tasks of daily life. The beauty lies in the journey, not just the destination. This philosophy is a powerful reminder of what it takes to endure and thrive in meaningful relationships.

In the context of parenthood, for example, there are countless repetitive and often tedious tasks—washing baby bottles, folding clothes, or tidying up after the chaos of the day. At first glance, these tasks may feel unremarkable, even burdensome. But when you shift your perspective, you begin to see the beauty in these small, daily acts of care. Each chore becomes an opportunity to provide for your child, to nurture their growth, and to contribute to their happiness. It's within these seemingly ordinary moments that extraordinary love is built.

The same principle applies to romantic relationships. There will be times when you need to consistently uplift and support your partner—through kind words, acts of service, or simply being present. While these efforts may feel routine, they are far from insignificant. The ability to make your partner smile, to encourage them after a tough day, or to show them love in small but consistent ways is a privilege, a blessing in itself.

The Beauty of the Process When we embrace the mundane tasks and responsibilities as essential components of the journey, we cultivate gratitude and resilience. We stop waiting for "perfect moments" to define our relationships and start appreciating the steady, day-to-day work that keeps them strong. The magic lies not in grand gestures, but in the quiet consistency of showing up for each other.

By falling in love with the process—whether it's folding laundry for your child or surprising your partner with their favorite coffee—you create a foundation of endurance and joy. The destination, whether it's raising a happy family or growing old with your partner, becomes a natural outcome of cherishing the steps along the way.

Expressing love through thoughtful actions and processes is a profound way to showcase care and connection. However, the trials of life often cloud our ability to appreciate the blessings embedded in each day. Take, for instance, the sound of a crying baby. For many parents, it can be a source of frustration or irritation, especially if the issue isn't resolved quickly. Yet, even in the midst of the noise, there's a profound blessing. First, the presence of a child is a gift in itself. Second, the child's ability to cry signifies life and vitality. Tragically, some parents who have experienced the loss of a child would give anything to hear that cry again. Recognizing these blessings allows us to shift our focus from frustration to gratitude.

Similarly, recurring challenges in relationships—like disagreements over household habits, such as folding and putting away clothes—are opportunities for growth. They provide a chance to improve communication, deepen understanding, and nurture a stronger bond. You might learn to express your concerns more effectively, while your partner might work on being more receptive. Ultimately, our perspective determines how we experience life's moments. Two people can face the same situation and emerge with entirely different attitudes—one optimistic and the other pessimistic. Which outlook will you choose?

It's often said that you'll find what you're looking for, so take care to cultivate a perspective that seeks gratitude and growth. By doing so, you not only enhance your own experience but also strengthen the relationships and connections that matter most.

Love Fuels the Journey

Endurance requires intentional effort and consistent practice (remember the 4 Ps). At its core, understanding your "why" is essential. Your "why" serves as the foundation of your strength, helping you shift your focus from the challenges you're enduring to the reason behind them.

For example, if you have a partner whom you love and care for and whom you envision marrying, that is your "why." Hold onto that vision because, in the midst of trials, it's important to remember why you're in the relationship in the first place. There are likely more good qualities about them than bad—otherwise, you wouldn't be with them.

If your partner loves you too, it's worth recognizing that they likely wouldn't intentionally hurt or harm you. This understanding is crucial. While it may feel at times like their actions are purposeful—especially if they've done something that frustrates you repeatedly—it's important to remember that we're all human. We make mistakes, get distracted, and sometimes fall short, even with the best intentions. Emotions can sometimes cloud our judgment, making us think our partner's actions are deliberate because they "should know better," mainly if we've addressed the issue multiple times. However, unlearning bad habits or adjusting behaviors takes time and grace. It's a tall task that requires patience and forgiveness on both sides.

Society often teaches us to chase immediate gratification, but true fulfillment comes from embracing the long journey and the rewards of delayed gratification. If enduring challenges were easy, everyone would achieve their goals effortlessly, whether it's building a successful relationship, becoming a millionaire, or sticking to a healthy lifestyle. Endurance is not about perfection; it's about perseverance, grace, and focusing on the "why" that keeps you committed to the process and the people you love.

Who is the ultimate example of staying true to their purpose out of love? **Jesus Christ.** He endured ridicule, beatings, being spit on, and ultimately crucifixion—all because He loved us enough to die in our place, giving us the opportunity for salvation.

Wow. Even in the midst of persecution, He asked God to forgive those who were harming Him, saying, *"Father, forgive them; for they know not what they do"* (Luke 23:34, KJV). Can you imagine responding to blatant rudeness or hurtful behavior from your partner the way Jesus responded—with love, compassion, and forgiveness?

That's the challenge we're called to embrace. Responding with love and compassion, even in difficult moments, is an essential part of being a leader in your relationships. As leaders, we must refuse to let the actions of others dictate our character or behavior.

As NBA Coach Monty Williams wisely said, *"Everything you want is on the other side of hard."* Growth requires doing things you've never done before, stretching yourself to evolve, and deepening your commitment to the relationships you value. Endurance in love is not easy, but it's worth every effort.

Rough Days

We all encounter days that are far from perfect—those times when we feel like our emotional reserves are depleted. Perhaps it's been a particularly tough day at work, family issues are weighing heavily, or life's many challenges are piling up. In such moments, it can be difficult to focus on the positive aspects of our relationships, especially when our partners' actions might seem frustrating. So, how can we navigate these situations effectively?

The first step is acknowledging that today is one of "those days"—a day when your emotional or mental capacity is stretched to its limits. I often think of this in terms of a metaphorical "cup" that represents my internal capacity to handle life's demands. On most days, my cup has plenty of room, allowing me to take on challenges and manage stress effectively. But there are days when it feels completely full, and any additional stress might lead to overwhelm. Recognizing this state is essential because it enables you to approach your day more mindfully. For instance, if my cup is already full, I consciously avoid engaging in potentially sensitive or conflict-heavy conversations. For example, after a long day with minimal sleep and back-to-back meetings, I wouldn't choose that moment to discuss minor frustrations, like how my wife smacks when she eats. My ability to communicate effectively and empathetically is diminished when my cup is overflowing.

WHEN YOUR CUP IS FULL, DON'T POUR.

On challenging days, it's crucial to communicate your emotional state to your partner. Let them know you're feeling drained, even if you don't want to go into detail. A simple, honest conversation like, "I'm feeling a bit stretched today—can we address this another time?" allows your partner to understand where you're coming from and adjust their expectations. Compassionate partners will often try to support you in reducing your stress or offloading burdens.

When your cup is full, it's important to find ways to recharge and regain perspective. Different outlets work for different people. Some might benefit from a long run, which allows them to clear their mind and release tension. Others might unwind by reading a good book with a glass of wine. Personally, I rely on talking to the Lord. Turning to the Lord allows me to unburden myself, gain renewed strength, and remember that all things work together for my good. Through prayer and reflection, I find clarity and the ability to refocus, viewing each new moment as an opportunity for growth.

Reframing how you see challenging days can make a significant difference. While difficult moments might feel overwhelming, they also present valuable opportunities to learn and grow in both your personal and relational dynamics. By approaching these situations with mindfulness, self-awareness, and intentional communication, you can handle them with grace and resilience. Perfection is a worthy goal, and even in the face of imperfection, each step you take toward handling life's challenges with purpose brings you closer to achieving it. With focus, patience, and intentionality, you can turn even the most trying days into moments of progress and connection.

Bible Time

Who: Jacob and Rachel
What: Endurance and Love
Where: Genesis 29:20-30

Jacob exemplifies how focusing on love can provide the strength to endure any challenge for someone you cherish. From the moment he saw Rachel, Jacob was captivated by her beauty and knew she was the woman he wanted to spend his life with. His dedication to marrying Rachel was so profound that he willingly agreed to work for seven years to earn her hand in marriage. His unwavering focus on his love for her made the long years of labor feel like only a few days to him:

> *"And Jacob served seven years for Rachel; and they seemed*
> *unto him but a few days, for the love he had to her"*
> *Genesis 29:20*

When the seven years of labor came to an end, Jacob was deceived by Laban, Rachel's father. Laban informed Jacob that it was customary for the eldest daughter, Leah, to marry first. As a result, Jacob was required to marry Leah instead of Rachel. Despite this betrayal, Jacob's commitment to Rachel never wavered. Determined to be with the woman he loved, Jacob married Leah and agreed to work an additional seven years to marry Rachel. His endurance and unwavering devotion highlight the depth of his love and dedication.

Jacob's story shows us that true love often requires patience, perseverance, and the ability to endure challenges. Endurance is not simply about waiting; it's about actively working toward a goal while holding onto faith and love through difficulties. For Jacob, the reward of being with Rachel far outweighed the hardships he endured.

His story is a reminder that enduring love means keeping the focus on the ultimate purpose, even when the process is longer or harder than expected. This enduring love mirrors how strong relationships are built today—through patience, effort, and commitment to the things and people that matter most. Jacob's example encourages us to persevere, trusting that the outcomes of love-driven endurance are worth the sacrifice.

If Jacob could work for 14 years to marry the woman he loved, can you commit to working daily on your relationships? Can you endure the tough days, focusing on love and the bond you share to nurture and strengthen what matters most?

CONSISTENCY WINS

THE POWER OF SHOWING UP EVERYDAY

C onsistency is more than just a word—it's a way of life. To exhibit the qualities of an exceptional partner, you must eat, sleep, and dream consistency. It's easy to show up for someone once or twice, but the real challenge lies in showing up every single day. Each day is its own unique journey, requiring focus and effort.

Imagine building a wall—not by obsessing over the finished structure but by concentrating on laying one perfect brick at a time. Will Smith famously used this analogy to highlight the importance of focusing on the small, purposeful actions that lead to larger accomplishments. Day by day, brick by brick, the wall eventually rises. This is the essence of consistency: the patience and dedication to repeat small, meaningful actions that, over time, create something extraordinary. Consider the difference between a casual basketball player and Steph Curry. Both may be able to make a single three-pointer, but the key distinction is who can do it consistently. Greatness is not just about how well you perform but how reliably you do it. The same applies to relationships. Your partner will expect you to show up in all aspects of life, day in and day out. That's what builds trust, connection, and success—not grand gestures but unwavering consistency.

CONSISTENCY IS LOVE IN MOTION.

Consistent Communication

Showing up consistently in a relationship often begins with communication. It's not just about talking but about making your partner feel understood, valued, and supported every single day. Once you've mastered the concept of "Wife Talk," as introduced earlier, you hold the keys to communicating effectively with your partner. But understanding isn't enough—you have to put it into practice daily and intentionally.

Consistency can be as simple as checking in regularly or sending a thoughtful good morning text. These small acts create a rhythm of connection that reinforces your presence in their life. Think of how parents talk to their children as they grow: when a baby is first born, they may not respond much, but parents instinctively speak to them with loving and nurturing words. These words, though seemingly one-sided at first, play a significant role in a child's emotional and cognitive development. Similarly, the words you choose in a relationship, whether grand or mundane, shape its foundation over time.

The power of words extends beyond just human relationships. Dr. Masaru Emoto, a Japanese researcher, explored how words, emotions, and intentions could influence the molecular structure of water. In his experiments, Emoto exposed water samples to various stimuli—such as positive and negative spoken words, written phrases, music, and prayers—and then froze the water to examine the resulting ice crystals. His findings were fascinating: positive words like "love" and "gratitude" created symmetrical, beautiful crystals, while negative words or harsh emotions resulted in chaotic, fragmented formations.

If words can have this kind of effect on water, imagine their impact on us, beings mainly made of water. While Emoto's research has faced some skepticism, the core message resonates: the energy behind our words has the power to shape environments, emotions, and relationships. In the context of communication, this means that consistent words of love, gratitude, and encouragement can nurture your partner, creating a sense of safety and connection. On the other hand, harsh or dismissive communication can damage trust and emotional closeness, much like those distorted crystals.

In relationships, your words don't need to be grandiose or perfect. It's not about saying the right thing once—it's about saying meaningful things consistently. Small gestures, like asking how their day went or expressing appreciation for their efforts, create ripples that accumulate over time. Think of these daily check-ins, affirmations, and acts of empathy as emotional investments. With every thoughtful word and intentional action, you're gaining emotional equity—building a reserve of trust, love, and connection that can carry your relationship through both ordinary days and challenging times. They may seem small, but these consistent efforts are the foundation of the trust and intimacy that sustain a relationship.

Consistency in communication isn't just about the words you choose but the intention behind them. A good morning text isn't just about saying hello; it's a daily reminder that you care and are present. Checking in about their day shows that you're not just hearing them but truly listening. These actions demonstrate that your love isn't fleeting or conditional—it's steady and reliable, day in and day out.

The beauty of showing up consistently is that it transforms ordinary moments into something extraordinary. Like the crystals in Emoto's research, the structure of your relationship becomes beautiful and strong, shaped by daily acts of care and communication. The key is to keep showing up—not perfectly, but consistently—because the little things you do every day are what makes love last.

Consistent Appreciation

Appreciation is one of the simplest yet most powerful ways to show up consistently in a relationship. It's easy to overlook the small, everyday acts of kindness and effort your partner contributes, but recognizing and valuing these moments can make a significant difference. Consistent appreciation isn't about extravagant gestures or over-the-top praise—it's about acknowledging the little things that often go unnoticed but mean so much.

Refer back to a time when you did something thoughtful for your partner—maybe you planned a special surprise, took care of a task they were stressed about, or supported them during a difficult moment. How did it feel when they genuinely expressed their appreciation for your effort? Their gratitude likely made you feel valued, seen, and motivated to continue showing up for them. Now, think about a time when the opposite happened—when you put in effort, but it went unnoticed or unacknowledged. You may have felt invisible or unimportant, as though your actions didn't matter.

This contrast highlights the power of consistent appreciation. Just as children seek acknowledgment for their efforts, adults also crave recognition to feel validated. When appreciation is withheld, it can lead to feelings of neglect or resentment, making it harder to maintain a healthy, supportive relationship. Conversely, when gratitude is consistently expressed, it reassures your partner that their contributions are meaningful and cherished.

The impact of consistent appreciation goes far beyond the moment. It sets off a ripple effect: when your partner feels valued, they're naturally more inclined to reciprocate and express gratitude for you. This creates a positive cycle of reinforcement, where both partners feel seen, loved, and inspired to keep showing up for each other. These small acts of appreciation build a foundation of emotional safety and mutual respect, fostering deeper intimacy over time.

Appreciation also works as a form of emotional currency in a relationship. Every time you express gratitude, you're depositing into an emotional bank account that strengthens your bond. These deposits can balance out inevitable withdrawals, such as conflicts, stressful times, or missteps, making it easier to navigate challenges together. When appreciation becomes a consistent habit, it builds a reserve of goodwill and positivity that sustains your relationship over time.

The power of appreciation isn't limited to words. Actions often speak louder. Small, thoughtful gestures, like surprising them with their favorite snack, leaving a heartfelt note, or offering to help when they seem overwhelmed, can convey appreciation just as effectively as spoken words. These actions show that you don't just recognize their contributions but also want to give back in meaningful ways.

In relationships, consistent appreciation doesn't mean showering your partner with constant praise or overcomplicating your efforts. It's about being intentional and genuine. A well-timed "thank you" or a small token of your gratitude can make your partner feel loved and respected every day. Over time, these consistent acts of appreciation help build a partnership rooted in mutual care and admiration.

How can we remember to always show appreciation? Sometimes, we assume our partners can read our minds or already know how we feel because we've said it before. However, whether they know it or not, it never hurts to communicate it again—it's always nice to hear. Women, in particular, often feel more appreciated when they can see and listen to it expressed consistently.

One way to ensure you're showing appreciation is by tying it to routines you both already engage in. For instance, if your partner cooks dinner daily, take a moment after the meal to express your gratitude for the effort and time it took to prepare. You can also show appreciation through actions, like offering to clean the dishes. This not only demonstrates your gratitude but also allows your partner to both see and hear how much you value them. Similarly, celebrate small wins, like when your partner saves a few dollars using a coupon at Target. Acknowledge how resourceful they are—it might seem insignificant to you, but it shows you notice and value their efforts. These small, consistent acts make a big difference in helping your partner feel seen and appreciated.

Consistently Keeping Your Promises

Keeping your word can be the foundation of trust in any relationship or, conversely, the source of insecurity and doubt when promises are broken.

Trust is a fragile construct, built over time but easily shattered with a single unfulfilled commitment. In relationships, being able to rely on your partner is quintessential, as it establishes a foundation of security and mutual respect. The phrase "Word is bond," popularized in New York, underscores the importance of honoring one's promises, reflecting the value society places on reliability and integrity. In relationships, the ability to depend on your partner is not just a virtue but a necessity. This principle extends across all types of relationships, from romantic partnerships to parent-child dynamics, shaping the way we perceive and interact with one another.

WORD IS BOND.

Take the example of children, particularly toddlers, and their interactions with their parents. As they grow, children at various developmental stages rely on their parents' words to guide their understanding of the world. Toddlers may place unconditional trust in their parents, while older children and teenagers begin to evaluate the consistency between words and actions. This trust is essential for building a sense of security and shapes their ability to form healthy relationships later in life. For young children, their parents' words are sacred. They lack the life experience to question or doubt what they are told, placing absolute faith in their caregivers. Imagine a scenario where a parent promises a child, "We'll get that toy next time." The first time this promise is made, the child believes it wholeheartedly. But if this same promise is repeated without fulfillment, the child begins to notice the disparity between words and actions. The trust they initially placed in their parent begins to erode. Over time, the broken promises about toys extend to other areas, leading to a broader sense of skepticism about their parent's reliability.

The same dynamic applies to adult relationships. In a romantic partnership, for instance, one broken promise—whether it's failing to show up for an important event, neglecting to follow through on shared goals, or simply not honoring day-to-day commitments—can create a fracture in the foundation of trust. While trust can often be repaired, rebuilding it requires effort, consistency, and time. Repeated breaches of trust can make the damage irreparable, leaving one or both parties questioning the future of the relationship.

The importance of keeping your word lies in the psychological safety it provides. Trustworthy behavior creates a sense of security, while unreliability fosters anxiety and doubt. Consider the emotional impact on a partner who cannot rely on their significant other. They may feel undervalued, disrespected, or even manipulated, leading to resentment and conflict. On the other hand, when a partner consistently follows through on promises, it reinforces the belief that they are dependable and committed, fostering a deeper emotional connection.

It's important to recognize that everyone faces challenges that can make it difficult to keep every promise. Life is unpredictable, and circumstances sometimes change beyond our control. However, the key is communication. If you know you cannot fulfill a promise, it is far better to address the issue openly and honestly than to remain silent or attempt to cover it up. Communicating your limitations demonstrates respect for the other person's feelings and shows that you value their trust enough to protect it, even when things don't go as planned.

For example, imagine a situation where a friend asks you to help them move on a particular day, and you agree. However, as the date approaches, unforeseen obligations make it impossible for you to assist. Rather than simply not showing up or canceling at the last minute, the responsible course of action is to inform your friend as soon as possible, apologize sincerely, and offer an alternative solution, such as helping on another day or contributing in another way. This proactive approach minimizes disappointment and preserves the trust in your relationship.

The ripple effects of broken promises often go unnoticed until the damage becomes significant. A parent who repeatedly fails to honor their commitments may inadvertently teach their children that promises are not important, perpetuating a cycle of unreliability. In romantic relationships, broken trust can lead to emotional withdrawal and decreased intimacy. So, how can we ensure that we keep our word? One effective way to ensure you keep your word is to practice mindful commitment. Before agreeing to something, take a moment to evaluate whether you truly have the time, resources, and ability to follow through. This approach prevents overcommitting and helps set realistic expectations. Another method is to use tools and strategies for accountability. Using a digital calendar, setting reminders on your phone, or even downloading productivity apps can keep you on track and make sure you don't miss a commitment. By tracking your commitments, you'll be better equipped to meet them. Additionally, make a conscious effort to prioritize smaller promises, not just significant commitments. Demonstrating reliability in everyday interactions builds a pattern of trustworthiness over time. For example, if you tell someone you'll call them at a certain time, make it a point to follow through consistently.

Ultimately, invest in personal development by taking time to look in the mirror and inventory your shortcomings. Reflect regularly on your ability to keep your word and identify areas for improvement, as accountability is strongly correlated with successfully keeping your word. Building self-awareness and developing better time management skills can significantly enhance your reliability, both in personal and professional contexts. The first step is to avoid overcommitting—set realistic expectations and aim to exceed them rather than making ambitious promises you cannot fulfill. If you're unsure whether you can deliver on a commitment, it's better to be honest upfront rather than risk disappointment later. Prioritizing accountability, such as keeping track of your commitments and setting reminders, ensures you follow through consistently. Following through requires organization and discipline, especially when juggling multiple responsibilities.

Accountability is not only a practical habit but also deeply rooted in spiritual teachings, offering further insight into the importance of keeping one's word. From a biblical perspective, keeping your word is deeply rooted in spiritual principles. Scriptures such as Matthew 5:37 emphasize the importance of integrity, teaching us to let our 'yes' mean 'yes' and our 'no' mean 'no.' This guidance underscores the value of honesty and reliability in our interactions. Proverbs 20:25 also warns against making promises lightly, reminding us of the weight and responsibility that come with our words. By keeping our word, we reflect God's faithfulness and build trust in our relationships, aligning our actions with the values of truth and commitment.

Finally, develop the habit of self-reflection and connect it with your commitment to accountability. Consider the promises you've made recently and assess how well you've honored them. Taking the time to look in the mirror and inventory your shortcomings allows you to identify areas for improvement and strengthens your ability to keep your word. Self-awareness is a powerful tool for personal growth, closely tied to accountability, and can help you build stronger, more reliable relationships.

Consistency with Time and Attention

Last but certainly not least, time and attention play a critical role in the dynamics of a relationship. Women often cherish the moments shared but are sometimes quick to notice and feel the absence when those moments are missing. This perception can create challenges for men, as the way men and women understand and value time and attention often differs significantly. Bridging this gap requires a deeper insight into these varying perspectives.

Let's explore an example to illustrate this difference. A man and a woman could spend an entire day cleaning their home, chatting about life, laughing, and working together as a team. The day might end with a relaxing movie on Netflix, accompanied by takeout—an enjoyable, shared experience. The next day, the man might decide to relax and watch football, only to hear his partner express that they haven't spent any quality time together. To the man, this can be baffling, even frustrating. In his mind, they just spent an entire day together. However, to his partner, the day before may not have fulfilled her need for meaningful connection.

The disconnect often lies in how time and attention are perceived. To many men, simply being in the same space, engaging in a shared activity, or enjoying casual conversation may count as quality time. It's togetherness, plain and simple. But for many women, time and attention are more nuanced. They seek intentionality—moments that feel significant and personal. Cleaning the house and watching a movie, while pleasant, might lack the emotional depth or romantic gesture that communicates, "You are special, and I cherish our connection." Women often value experiences that are infused with thoughtfulness. They envision dates, surprises, or moments that allow them to feel prioritized. It's not just about being together physically but creating occasions where the focus is entirely on nurturing the relationship. These moments affirm their worth and the strength of the bond.

This dynamic bears a striking resemblance to interactions with children. Imagine a parent spending the whole day with their child, taking care of errands, attending appointments, and tackling household chores. From the parent's perspective, they've been present the entire time. But from the child's point of view, those hours may not feel like "quality time." They crave undivided attention—whether it's playing their favorite game, reading a book together, or simply sitting down and listening to their stories without distractions. Children value moments where they feel truly seen and heard. Similarly, in a relationship, a woman's desire for quality time often centers on the emotional connection that such moments foster. It's not about the quantity of time but the quality and intention behind it.

As men, this realization may *feel* overwhelming or an unfair expectation. Fortunately, it's actually an opportunity to deepen our understanding and strengthen the relationship. Empathizing with your partner's vantage point will make them feel seen, heard, and loved. Here are some practical ways to emphasize the importance of time and attention:

1. **Be Intentional**. Quality time doesn't have to involve lavish gestures. It's about the thought and effort behind the moment. Planning a simple dinner where you focus solely on each other, going for a walk, or creating a shared experience can make all the difference. Intentionality shows that you've prioritized her needs and the relationship.

2. **Communicate and Clarify** Open dialogue about what quality time means to each of you is essential. Share your perspectives and expectations, and listen without judgment. Understanding

her unique needs allows you to align your actions with her vision of connection.

3. **Incorporate Variety** Routine can sometimes dull the spark. Introducing variety, whether it's trying a new activity, visiting a favorite spot, or engaging in her interests, keeps the relationship dynamic and fresh. It also demonstrates that you're willing to invest effort in creating meaningful experiences.

4. **Learn and Adapt** Relationships thrive on growth and adaptability. As you spend more time together, you'll learn more about her preferences and how she feels most loved. Use this knowledge to tailor your efforts and create a rhythm that works for both of you.

Ultimately, time and attention in relationships boil down to being present. Presence is about more than just physical proximity—it's about emotional engagement and intentional focus. Even though perspectives may be different, the goal is to meet in the middle—to create a relationship where both partners feel valued and fulfilled.

THE POWER OF BONDING

FROM BABIES TO PARTNERS

B aby bonding at birth is one of the most important aspects of a newborn's development, fostering emotional, social, and physical growth. This nurturing connection between a parent and child has profound, lasting effects, influencing not only the child's immediate well-being but also their lifelong ability to form relationships. Baby bonding involves practices such as skin-to-skin contact, promptly responding to the baby's needs, maintaining eye contact, talking or singing softly, playing, and cuddling. These actions create a secure attachment, which is essential for a child's development. Here, we delve into the impacts of baby bonding and explore how these principles can be extended to deepen adult relationships, emphasizing the power of physical touch and emotional connection.

The Benefits of Baby Bonding

Emotional Security: Early bonding creates a foundation of trust and attachment that influences the baby's relationships throughout life.

Skin-to-skin contact, especially in the early days, reassures the baby of their safety and builds a sense of security.

Stress Reduction: Physical closeness and responsive caregiving help regulate the baby's cortisol (stress hormone) levels. This fosters a calm and stable emotional state, reducing anxiety and promoting resilience.

Neural Growth: Positive interactions like cuddling, eye contact, and talking stimulate the baby's brain by fostering neural connections. These connections are crucial for cognitive development and emotional regulation.

Immune System Support: Physical touch, such as skin-to-skin contact, strengthens the baby's immune system and contributes to healthy growth.

If bonding has such monumental effects on a newborn's progression, imagine the profound impact it can have on adult relationships when applied correctly. The principles of baby bonding—physical touch, emotional attentiveness, and consistent engagement—are equally powerful in cultivating intimacy and connection between partners.

Strengthening Relationships Through Bonding Principles

Just as a baby thrives on emotional and physical attention, so do adults in their relationships. Women, like men, require emotional and physical nurturing to feel valued and connected. Deepening the emotional connection between partners enhances the physical aspects of a relationship, creating a positive feedback loop of intimacy and satisfaction.

Beyond Sex: While physical touch is often associated with sex, it encompasses so much more. Holding hands, touching a shoulder during a conversation, or maintaining eye contact during a shared moment all reinforce a sense of connection. These small actions communicate care, engagement, and presence, which are essential in any relationship.

Physical touch is a love language for many and a cornerstone of bonding. Touch communicates emotions that words cannot, fostering closeness and trust. Here are a few ways physical touch strengthens relationships:

- **Cuddling and Holding Hands:** Whether it's holding hands in public or cuddling on the couch, these actions demonstrate affection and security.

- **Touch During Conversations:** Placing a hand on your partner's shoulder or leg during a conversation shows attentiveness and engagement. It's a non-verbal way of saying, "I'm here, and I care."

- **Hugs and Kisses:** Daily gestures of affection, like a hug when you reunite after a long day, create a sense of belonging and intimacy.

Bonding isn't just about physical touch; it's also about emotional presence. Responding to your partner's emotional needs is akin to responding to a baby's cries—it's about showing up and being attuned to their feelings.

- **Listening Actively:** Pay attention when your partner speaks, maintaining eye contact and showing genuine interest. This mirrors the way a parent engages with a baby during bonding moments.

- **Small Acts of Kindness:** Thoughtful gestures, like making breakfast for your partner or sending an encouraging text, show that you're thinking about them.

Cultivating Lifelong Connection

Just as baby bonding involves responsiveness, physical touch, and emotional attentiveness, adult relationships flourish under the same principles. Consider the parallels:

- **Skin-to-Skin Contact vs. Holding Hands:** Skin-to-skin contact reassures a baby of their safety, while holding hands in public creates a sense of unity and pride in a relationship.

- **Responding to Cries vs. Listening Actively:** When a baby cries, a parent's prompt response builds trust. Similarly, listening actively and responding to your partner's emotional needs strengthens your bond.

- **Cuddling vs. Daily Affection:** Cuddling helps a baby feel secure, and consistent daily affection, like hugs and kisses, has the same effect on a partner.

Bonding doesn't stop after the newborn stage or the honeymoon phase of a relationship. It's an ongoing process that requires intentionality and effort. By incorporating the principles of baby bonding into your relationship—physical touch, attentiveness, and responsiveness—you can create a relationship that feels as safe and nurturing as a parent's embrace.

Remember, bonding is about building a foundation of trust and love, whether it's with a newborn or a lifelong partner. It's the little things—holding hands, maintaining eye contact, or sharing a laugh—that weave the fabric of connection, making your bond unbreakable.

The Importance of Being Available

Availability is the foundation of meaningful connection in any relationship, whether between a parent and child or romantic partners. Being available means more than just being physically present—it requires emotional presence, attentiveness, and a willingness to engage.

Emotional availability involves being open to your partner's feelings, needs, and concerns. When you consistently show that you are there to listen and support, you foster trust and deepen the bond. This mirrors the way a parent responds to a baby's cries, reinforcing a sense of safety and connection.

- **Active Engagement:** Show your partner they have your full attention by setting aside distractions like phones or work during important conversations. Eye contact, nodding, and thoughtful responses can make them feel heard and valued.

- **Validation:** Acknowledge your partner's emotions, even if you don't fully understand or agree. Statements like, "I can see why you feel that way," show empathy and openness.

Physical presence plays a key role in maintaining intimacy. While life's responsibilities often pull us in different directions, making time for physical closeness, even in small ways, keeps the connection alive.

- **Quality Time:** Schedule moments to connect, like a regular date night or an evening walk. Consistent availability demonstrates that your relationship is a priority.

- **Physical Proximity:** Simple acts like sitting next to each other while watching TV or working together in the same space create opportunities for spontaneous moments of closeness.

Much like how a baby relies on the constant presence of a caregiver to feel secure, romantic partners thrive on the reassurance of availability. When both partners feel that they can rely on each other emotionally and physically, it strengthens trust and promotes long-term intimacy. Being available is an act of love that communicates, "I'm here for you, no matter what." This commitment creates the emotional and physical safety required for deeper bonding and a resilient relationship. Ultimately, availability is a cornerstone of the power of bonding, allowing relationships to thrive through trust, presence, and consistent engagement.

The Hidden Costs of Disconnection

Failing to constantly water the emotional and physical portions of your relationship will impact the sexual intimacy level of your relationship. When emotional needs go unmet, it can lead to feelings of neglect, resentment, and a gradual erosion of trust and connection. Similarly, a lack of physical affection—like hugs, touches, or simple gestures of closeness—can make a relationship feel distant and transactional rather than nurturing and loving.

Disconnection often begins subtly, with busy schedules, stress, or distractions pulling partners apart. Over time, this can create a cycle where emotional and physical intimacy fade, making it harder to reconnect.

Without the consistent practice of bonding behaviors, partners may feel isolated even when physically together.

Rekindling Connection: Fostering intimacy requires daily "warming up" through small, intentional acts. Think of nurturing your relationship like preparing for a satisfying meal—you wouldn't bake a dish in a cold oven. Similarly, emotional and physical connection requires effort throughout the day. Gentle touches as you pass each other, sharing moments of laughter, or holding hands while walking create an atmosphere of closeness. These actions ensure that partners feel valued and connected, making deeper physical and emotional intimacy a natural extension rather than an isolated event.

YOU WOULDN'T BAKE A DISH IN A COLD OVEN—
So don't expect intimacy without warming it up.

The consequences of disconnection extend beyond the couple's relationship. It can affect overall happiness, mental health, and even how partners interact with children, friends, or colleagues. The ripple effect of unaddressed disconnection can make rebuilding the bond feel overwhelming.

However, the principles of bonding offer a way back. By prioritizing emotional attentiveness, small physical gestures, and consistent engagement, couples can rekindle their connection. Just as bonding creates a secure foundation for a baby's development, it can restore and strengthen the bond between partners. In the same way that babies thrive on love and touch, adult relationships flourish when nurtured with care and intention.

The power of bonding lies in its ability to create security, trust, and joy. Whether it's through a touch, a kind word, or a shared moment of laughter, these small acts can rebuild and sustain a connection, ensuring relationships remain strong and fulfilling.

One-Word Reflection:

What's one word you want your partner to feel every time they're with you?

FEED ME

PROVIDING AS PURPOSE

R emember the song "What You Won't Do for Love" by Bobby Caldwell? This classic R&B hit captures the depths we'll go to for love, from romantic connections to the unwavering devotion of parental care. As parents, you'd do whatever it takes to ensure your children have food on the table. You'll work long hours, sacrifice your own comfort, and even go without so that they never have to. That same instinct—to nurture, protect, and provide—should extend to your partner, the person with whom you share your life and dreams. Just as providing for your children reflects your love and responsibility, providing for your partner is a way to sustain and deepen your connection.

Most people tend to focus on financial contributions when it comes to providing, and while finances are an important foundation, there's so much more that partners and children require for their well-being. It encompasses emotional, physical, and spiritual support as well. It's about creating a safe and abundant environment for your loved ones to flourish. In romantic relationships, it's about cultivating a heart of giving. When approached with a willing and joyful spirit, providing becomes a way of honoring the connection you share and ensuring its growth.

PROVISION ISN'T ABOUT MONEY — IT'S ABOUT CREATING SAFETY.

Providing as a Core Instinct

There's a unique joy in ensuring the well-being of those you love. This drive, rooted in our very survival instincts, compels us to do whatever it takes to protect and nurture our families. For children, this manifests in the security of knowing their needs will always be met. They trust their parents completely, never worrying about where their next meal will come from. That same peace of mind is what your partner deserves—a sense of safety and unwavering support, even during life's uncertainties.

There's something deeply fulfilling about giving your best to those you love. When you know the person you love doesn't have to worry about where their next meal is going to come from, you receive a special peace. This desire is innate in many people, a reflection of the human instinct to ensure the well-being of their tribe. Whether it's packing a lunch for your child or picking up your partner's favorite snack after a long day, these acts of provision carry a profound emotional weight. Importantly, this instinct to provide can be cultivated and learned. Men who may not naturally lean into this role can take steps to align themselves with this purpose, committing to doing whatever it takes to provide the security and care their families need. This extends to offering women a sense of security in a world that often tries to strip that from them at every angle. Ensuring that your partner feels safe, protected, and valued creates a foundation of trust and stability that allows relationships to thrive. By fostering this mindset and passing these values down to future generations, we ensure that all men are equipped to embrace the duty of provision, creating a legacy of love and responsibility.

> **Provision**: The act of giving or making something available to people who need or want it

In the context of parenting, providing often feels non-negotiable. You don't question whether you'll do what's necessary to keep your children safe and nurtured. The same principle applies to romantic relationships, but here's the difference: while providing for your kids may feel obligatory, **providing for your partner can be approached as an intentional act of love**. This subtle shift—from obligation to desire—transforms provision into an expression of devotion.

Adapting to Modern Realities

Providing today looks different. While the financial stability of a long-term job is less common, modern provision often combines strategic financial planning with emotional and relational care. While one partner may not be solely responsible for material resources, the desire to give your best should still exist. Back in the day, a man could stay on a job for 30 years, and that would be enough to provide a place to stay, food, and even a little excess to enjoy life. Today, however, there must be a conscious effort to strive for more. This might include pursuing multiple streams of income, advancing in your career, or investing and budgeting wisely. While your current ecosystem plays a part, when there's a will, there's a way. In the meantime, provision isn't limited to finances. It could mean offering emotional support after a stressful workday, being an active listener, or sharing responsibilities to lighten the load. Financial provision can also adapt to modern realities, such as budgeting effectively, pursuing side income streams like freelancing or small business ventures, or investing in skills and education to improve earning potential. These efforts demonstrate a commitment to securing a stable and thriving environment for your family.

Small gestures carry significant weight in this dynamic. For example, consider arranging a weekly or monthly date night to celebrate your relationship. It doesn't have to be extravagant—what matters is the intention behind it. Perhaps you send your partner lunch at work through a delivery service, so it's one less thing they need to think about. These acts communicate care and thoughtfulness, reinforcing the bond between you.

Obligation vs Desire

Providing becomes transformative when it's driven by desire rather than duty. Now, men, there's nothing worse than feeling like your partner expects you to handle everything financially without recognition or support. However, the reality is these expectations often exist, whether verbalized or not. Instead of focusing on the expectations, shift your attention to the desire within to be the man you're destined to be. This doesn't mean that every act of provision will feel effortless; sometimes, it's hard work. Imagine working 12-hour days to save up for that one toy your child has been dreaming about for the last six months. The smile and happiness they'll exhibit on Christmas morning or their birthday when they open the gift will make every effort worthwhile. That moment will bring you a joy that's unmatched, reminding you why providing from the heart matters so much. When your motivation stems from a heartfelt desire to see your loved ones thrive, it shifts the experience. It's the difference between begrudgingly working late and choosing to do so because you know it will contribute to a better life for your family. It's the difference between resenting the effort it takes to plan a date night and finding joy in creating a moment of connection.

This mindset doesn't just benefit your partner—it also nurtures you. When you view provision as an extension of love, it fosters a sense of purpose and fulfillment. Doing this out of desire removes the opportunity to hold resentment toward your partner for paying for things. It also makes it less likely for you to try to control your partner just because you're the financial breadwinner. Instead, things need to be done out of love and not based on what will be given in return. The joy of giving, especially when it's received with gratitude, becomes its own reward.

Provision Liberates

When you have a desire to provide for your partner's needs, it's liberating for your loved one. It not only strengthens your bond, but it also encourages a sense of stability. Your partner will recognize that as a commitment that you're in for the long haul. It's like consistently investing in the S&P 500. Yes, there's a financial component, but you're investing in your future, and the returns will be exponential. Now, it may not translate to more financial dollars, but it may be returned in other areas like peace, a stronger partnership, and a support system to help you reach your goals.

When your actions stem from a heartfelt desire to see your partner and family thrive, there's no room for bitterness over what you've given. Providing out of love fosters joy and fulfillment, knowing that each effort contributes to the well-being of those you care about. This mindset helps your partner feel more secure and supported as they recognize your commitment to their well-being. For instance, ensuring monthly bills are paid on time creates a predictable and stable environment that relieves stress. Similarly, surprising your partner with a thoughtful gift, like a book they've been eyeing, reinforces emotional connection and care. These tangible acts of provision make your partner feel valued and supported, fostering a stronger and more trusting relationship. Instead, provision becomes a way to build a stronger partnership based on mutual respect and shared goals. When done with genuine love, it creates an environment where both partners feel valued, supported, and empowered to thrive together.

Providing Beyond Finances

Provision is not solely about financial contributions; it encompasses emotional, physical, and spiritual support that fosters a thriving relationship. Here are some ways to provide beyond finances, each contributing uniquely to the bond between you and your partner:

1. **Emotional Support**: Being a source of comfort and understanding is one of the most profound ways to provide for your partner. Listen attentively when they share their feelings or struggles. Create a space where they feel safe to express themselves without fear of judgment. For example, after a challenging day, ask, "How can I support you right now?" or simply offer a reassuring hug. This builds trust and emotional intimacy.

2. **Quality Time**: Investing time in your partner is a vital form of provision. Plan activities that allow you to connect, whether it's going for a walk or taking a dancing class. Quality time signals that your partner is a priority and strengthens the emotional connection.

3. **Physical Presence**: Being physically present during critical moments shows your partner that you are dependable. For example, accompanying them to a doctor's appointment or helping with household chores demonstrates care and shared responsibility.

4. **Spiritual Growth**: Providing spiritual support can bring a deeper sense of connection and purpose to your relationship. This might involve praying together, attending religious services, or exploring shared values and goals. Encouraging each other's personal growth creates a strong foundation for the relationship.

5. **Words of Affirmation**: Expressing love and appreciation through words is another powerful way to provide. Compliment their efforts, acknowledge their achievements, and remind them how much they mean to you. A simple "I'm proud of you" or "Thank you for everything you do" can uplift and motivate your partner.

6. **Acts of Service**: Small gestures of assistance go a long way in showing care. Whether it's running an errand, preparing their favorite meal, or handling a task they've been dreading, these acts demonstrate thoughtfulness and reduce stress for your partner.

When you provide in these ways, you're not just contributing to your partner's well-being—you're nurturing the relationship itself. These forms of provision create a balanced, supportive dynamic where love and respect flourish. By going beyond finances, you demonstrate that provision is about fostering a holistic sense of security and care, ensuring your partner feels cherished in every aspect of life.

Bible Time

Who: Boaz
What: Provision with love, dignity, and protection
Where: Ruth 2–4

The story of Boaz and Ruth highlights how provision goes beyond financial support to include care, protection, and respect. Ruth, a widow, chose to stay with her mother-in-law, Naomi, after they both lost their husbands. To provide for them, Ruth began gathering leftover grain in the fields during harvest. Boaz, the landowner, noticed her hard work and ensured she had extra grain, offering her safety and kindness.

Boaz didn't stop at providing food; he went further by giving Ruth dignity and a sense of security. He treated her with respect and made sure she felt valued. Eventually, Boaz took on the role of redeemer by marrying Ruth, ensuring stability and a future for her and Naomi.

This story demonstrates that provision isn't just about material wealth but about showing care and creating an environment where others feel safe and supported. Boaz's actions remind us that true provision is about seeing a need and responding with love and intentionality. As Proverbs 11:25 (KJV) states, "The liberal soul shall be made fat: and he that watereth shall be watered also himself." Boaz's generosity reflects this principle, as his care for Ruth ultimately brought blessings and fulfillment to his own life.

TIME SERVED

STRENGTHENING RELATIONSHIPS THROUGH SELFLESS ACTS

In relationships, issues often arise around power dynamics—who's in control and making decisions. Instead of engaging in a battle for dominance, the focus should shift to a contest of service: who can out-serve the other. True leadership in a relationship, especially for men, lies not in exerting authority but in embracing a servant's heart. The goal should be to make your partner's journey through life as pleasant and fulfilling as possible. While society may depict leadership as being in control, the Bible offers a different perspective: "But he that is greatest among you shall be your servant" (Matthew 23:11). Jesus Christ, who held all power on earth, exemplified this by choosing to serve—washing the feet of His disciples and meeting the needs of others. Leadership, at its core, is about humility, sacrifice, and the courage to do what others shy away from. In both parenting and relationships, this same servant's heart is essential. Whether it's prioritizing your partner's needs over your own, actively listening even in moments of disagreement, or offering unwavering support in tough times, serving others is the ultimate expression of love and true leadership.

Redefining Leadership in Relationships

Leadership is frequently misunderstood and often equated with dominance or control. However, true leadership, especially within the context of romantic relationships, is not about exerting power but rather about embracing responsibility. At its core, leadership in a relationship emphasizes protection, care, and provision. It requires a selfless commitment to the well-being of the partnership, prioritizing the needs of the union over individual desires. This nuanced view of leadership invites us to rethink traditional gender dynamics, understanding them not as rigid roles but as complementary strengths.

Whether we like it or not, gender dynamics play a significant role in relationships, especially in moments of crisis or challenge. For instance, if there's a burglar breaking into the home, nine times out of ten, it's expected that the man will step forward to protect his family. Similarly, when a woman feels disrespected, she often looks to her partner to defend her honor and stand by her side. These scenarios aren't about assigning value to one gender over the other but rather acknowledging natural tendencies and societal expectations that have evolved over time.

A man who embraces leadership within his relationship recognizes these dynamics and willingly accepts the accompanying responsibilities. He understands that leadership is not a privilege to wield but a challenge to embrace. It often requires putting aside personal wants or conveniences for the greater good of the relationship. This could mean taking initiative during difficult times, providing stability during uncertainty, or offering unwavering support when his partner needs reassurance.

LEADERSHIP ISN'T ABOUT BEING IN CHARGE—IT'S ABOUT SHOWING UP WHEN IT'S HARDEST.

This sense of leadership extends naturally into parenting, where the role of a father as a leader becomes even more crucial. For example, a father teaching his son how to be a gentleman—by modeling behaviors such as opening doors or pulling out chairs for women—illustrates leadership in action. These seemingly small gestures teach values like respect, consideration, and thoughtfulness. By demonstrating these traits in his daily interactions, a father sets an example for his children, reinforcing the idea that true leadership is about serving others with dignity and kindness.

It's important to recognize that not everyone agrees a man should lead in a relationship. Many people believe that men and women should share all responsibilities equally. While that view has merit, it's worth considering that two things can be equal but still serve different purposes. For example, a pound of sugar and a pound of salt weigh the same and might even look similar, but they have very different uses. In the same way, men and women bring unique strengths to a relationship. Leadership doesn't make one better than the other; it's simply about fulfilling different roles that work together to create balance. As the Bible states in Ephesians 5:23 (KJV): "For the husband is the head of the wife, even as Christ is the head of the church; and he is the saviour of the body." This verse highlights the idea of leadership as a role of care, responsibility, and sacrificial love, modeled after Christ's relationship with the church.

True leadership in a relationship is not about superiority but about service. It calls for a balance of strength and compassion, decisiveness and empathy. By understanding this complexity, men can create an environment where their partners feel safe, valued, and supported. Leadership, in this sense, becomes a cornerstone of a thriving partnership rooted in mutual respect and a shared vision for the future.

Service in Action

The beauty of relationships lies in the endless opportunities to serve your partner. Whether through grand gestures or small acts of kindness, the impact can be monumental in strengthening your bond. Serving daily requires attentiveness, intentionality, and a willingness to prioritize your partner's needs.

First and foremost, active listening is key. When you genuinely listen, you can uncover exactly what your partner truly needs. Let's imagine your partner has been under a lot of stress at work and feels drained from her daily workouts. By paying attention to her concerns, you might discover that she could benefit from a moment of relaxation. Perhaps you could offer her a soothing massage at home, or, if that's not your forte, surprise her with a gift card to a professional massage parlor. These thoughtful actions not only alleviate her stress but also show that you're attuned to her well-being.

If your partner typically handles the cooking, consider stepping into the kitchen to prepare a meal for her. It doesn't have to be fancy—what matters is the effort and thoughtfulness. Follow it up by doing the dishes and giving her a well-deserved break from her routine. These actions not only lighten her load but also demonstrate your willingness to contribute and care for her. Similarly, you might notice that she's feeling overwhelmed by a busy schedule or the demands of daily life. Step in by organizing her day or taking over a task she usually handles, like running errands or tidying up the house. This creates space for her to relax, recharge, or focus on something she loves.

Serving doesn't always involve physical tasks. Sometimes it's about emotional and spiritual support. Take the lead in praying with her or for her, offering encouragement during tough times. A kind word, a heartfelt note, or even just being present in a quiet moment can uplift her spirit and remind her that she's not alone. When she feels supported emotionally and spiritually, the foundation of your relationship grows stronger.

The Bible provides a timeless model for serving your partner. Ephesians 5:25 (KJV) states: "Husbands, love your wives, even as Christ also loved the church, and gave himself for it." This verse highlights the self-sacrificial love that should define a husband's role in a relationship. Just as Christ gave Himself for the church, men are called to serve their partners selflessly, prioritizing their needs above their own desires. For example, if your partner has a long-standing dream or goal, supporting her pursuit—even if it requires you to make sacrifices—can be a profound way to serve.

So, how can you serve your partner on a daily basis? Relationships are unique, and each person has their own needs and love languages. Take a moment to reflect and write down some ways you can serve your partner. What tasks does your partner usually handle that you could take over occasionally? What are some small gestures, like making coffee, running errands, or writing a love note, that might brighten her day? Has she mentioned needing help with something recently, even if it seemed minor? How can you create moments for her to relax, recharge, or enjoy something she loves? How can you pray for her or encourage her in her personal or spiritual growth?

By actively seeking opportunities to serve, you strengthen not just your relationship but also your character. Big or small, every act of service is a step toward a stronger and more loving partnership. The key is consistency and a heart willing to give without expecting anything in return.

Out-Serving Each Other

Serving your partner not only nurtures their well-being but also creates a ripple effect that enriches your relationship. When you serve selflessly, you inspire your partner to do the same, fostering a culture of gratitude, mutual respect, and selflessness. This dynamic isn't about keeping score or competing to see who can outdo the other; it's about giving from a place of love and genuine care for your partner's happiness and growth. True service stems from a desire to uplift and support, not from an expectation of something in return.

LOVE SHOWS UP. IT DOESN'T KEEP RECEIPTS.

When serving becomes transactional—when you do something solely with the hope or expectation that your partner will reciprocate—it loses its power. This tit-for-tat mentality often leads to resentment or disappointment when your actions aren't acknowledged or repaid in kind. True selflessness requires letting go of the need for validation and focusing on the benefit of your partner. Leadership in service is about setting the standard, even when no one notices. It's about doing the right thing because it strengthens your bond and enriches your partner's life, not because you're seeking recognition or reward.

Serving isn't always met with gratitude or recognition, especially at first. Consider a server at a restaurant—they are expected to deliver exceptional service regardless of how they are treated. Recognition is like tips—it's not guaranteed, but it's nice to have. Their role is to provide, not to demand appreciation. The same principle applies to relationships. There will be moments when your efforts go unnoticed or unacknowledged, but greatness often requires thankless work. Think about the late Kobe Bryant, who spent countless hours in the gym perfecting his craft when no one was watching. He wasn't motivated by applause but by an intrinsic desire to be the best. In relationships, this same mindset can serve as a catalyst for change. Your selflessness can inspire your partner to follow suit, creating a virtuous cycle of love and service.

When you serve with humility and dedication, you create an environment where gratitude flourishes. Over time, your actions will naturally encourage your partner to reflect on their own contributions, not out of obligation but because they feel inspired by your example. The beauty of serving lies in its transformative power—it doesn't just strengthen your partner or your relationship; it shapes you into a better, more compassionate person. In this way, serving is both a gift to your partner and a growth opportunity for yourself, one that leads to deeper connection and fulfillment.

When Service Becomes Strength

You might catch yourself thinking, *"Why should I serve? Wouldn't it be better to be the one served?"* It's like looking at a newborn and saying, *"They've got the dream life—no responsibilities, no stress, just being cared for."* But here's the catch: while being served might seem appealing, it can't compare to the joy of giving. Babies may have their needs met, but they miss out on the incredible opportunity to make someone else's day better. Serving isn't about what you lose; it's about what you gain—a sense of purpose, fulfillment, and the ability to create something meaningful in your relationship.

Serving is liberating. It frees you from the constant pressure of focusing on your own needs and gives you the unique opportunity to put a smile on someone else's face. There's an indescribable joy in knowing you've made someone's day better, no matter how small the gesture. Over time, as you practice selflessness, you'll begin to recognize the resilience you've cultivated. Acts of service, repeated over and over, build a strength within you that you might not have thought possible. The things in your life that once felt all-consuming and urgent begin to take a backseat. You start prioritizing what truly matters—love, connection, and purpose—things you may have overlooked before.

Serving also forces self-evaluation. It prompts you to question your motives and consider why you do the things you do. Are your actions driven by love or by a desire for validation? This reflection helps you align your life with values that genuinely bring fulfillment. Through serving, you'll begin to notice not just changes in your relationships but in your personal growth. You'll discover a deeper sense of purpose—not just in your relationship but in life itself. Serving reminds you that you are part of something bigger and that your actions have meaning beyond yourself.

The Bible reminds us in Acts 20:35 that "It is more blessed to give than to receive." Serving aligns with this principle, offering blessings that aren't always tangible but are undeniably transformative. And as Galatians 6:7 says, "For whatsoever a man soweth, that shall he also reap." By serving selflessly, you sow seeds of kindness, love, and generosity, and in due season, you'll reap the rewards. They may not come in the form you expect, but they will show up—often in other areas of life, through deeper connections, unexpected opportunities, or a newfound peace and joy.

Ultimately, serving doesn't diminish you; it enriches you. It builds resilience, fosters self-reflection, strengthens your character, and gives your life and relationships deeper meaning. The act of giving is its own reward, and the ripple effects of your selflessness will come back to you in ways you could never imagine. So, while it might feel easier to wish for a life of being served, true growth and joy come when you choose to serve others with a willing and open heart.

A GREAT RELATIONSHIP DOESN'T JUST MEET EXPECTATIONS—IT EXCEEDS THEM.

Reflection Time:

How can you serve your partner better? Use the below questions to identify opportunities where you can enhance your relationship:

- What are some ways you can out-serve your partner today?

- Can you think of a time when serving your partner brought unexpected joy to you? How did it impact your relationship?

- How do you handle moments when your acts of service go unnoticed? Could this be an area for personal growth?

- What small but meaningful gesture could you do today to make your partner's life a little easier?

In life, there's a difference between good and great relationships. In a good relationship, you treat others the way you want to be treated. In a great relationship, you go beyond your own expectations, striving to be the best partner you can be and exceeding even what you hope to receive in return.

LOVE WITHOUT STRINGS

THE ART OF LOVING WITHOUT EXPECTATIONS

H ave you ever seen a medication commercial with a list of side effects ten times longer than the benefits it promises to deliver? Sometimes, that's how we approach love—overloaded with expectations and conditions that outweigh the joy it's meant to bring. We're drawn to the idea of what we think love should look like, attaching strings and anticipating specific returns for the affection we offer. But this kind of transactional love is neither fulfilling nor enduring.

True love should be unconditional, free from expectations or demands. It should mirror the innate and inexplicable love a mother feels when she first holds her newborn baby. The baby hasn't done anything to earn her love—there are no achievements or actions to validate it. Yet, the love is overwhelming, instinctual, and absolute. This is the essence of unconditional love.

Unconditional love is a pure, selfless form of affection and care that transcends circumstances and conditions. It's the act of loving someone entirely for who they are, not for what they do or how they make you feel. It does not require the other person to meet specific standards, fulfill expectations, or reciprocate in a particular way. At its core, unconditional love is a commitment—a deliberate choice to accept and cherish another person, even in the face of their flaws, mistakes, or limitations.

This form of love is not about perfection or performance; it's about connection. It's the kind of love that forms the foundation for lasting, meaningful relationships, offering both freedom and security. By embracing unconditional love, we move beyond transactional relationships into a deeper, more authentic connection that reflects the very best of what love is meant to be.

Expectations

Society places countless expectations on what relationships should look like. From movies to social media to billboard advertisements, the message is clear: relationships are about what you should *receive*. Whether it's extravagant gestures, constant affirmation, or someone who checks every box on an imaginary "ideal partner" list, the focus often skews toward personal gratification rather than mutual growth. This one-sided narrative sets people up for disappointment because it fosters unrealistic expectations that no real relationship can meet.

Having desires and preferences in a relationship is perfectly normal—it's okay to want certain things from your partner. However, it's equally important to approach the relationship with flexibility and a willingness to meet your partner where they are. Consider this: You've always envisioned being with someone who can cook, but your spouse prefers to eat out. You could view this as a frustration and dwell on what's missing, or you could reframe it as an opportunity for connection. Why not make cooking a shared activity? Spending time together in the kitchen, exploring recipes, and creating meals as a team can turn a potential conflict into a bonding experience. As the Bible says, *"Iron sharpeneth iron; so a man sharpeneth the countenance of his friend"* (Proverbs 27:17).

LOVE CAN'T GROW WHERE ENTITLEMENT TAKES ROOT.

This principle applies beyond cooking. Unrealistic expectations often arise in areas like communication, affection, or time management. While it's healthy to communicate your needs, relationships thrive when there's a balance of giving and receiving. Parenthood offers a valuable parallel: a parent's love for their child is unwavering and freely given, not based on what the child does or doesn't do. Similarly, in relationships, focusing on giving rather than expecting fosters trust and security, allowing both partners to grow.

This selfless love is rooted in Christianity. The Bible commands us to love one another as Christ loves us—unconditionally and sacrificially. Jesus said, *"This is my commandment, That ye love one another, as I have loved you"* (John 15:12). Just as God's love for us is not contingent on our actions, our love for our partners should reflect the same grace and generosity. Love becomes more than a feeling; it is a deliberate choice and commitment.

When love is rooted in giving—whether through time, patience, or support—it creates space for both partners to thrive. True connection comes from partnership, where two people work together to create something greater than themselves. By embracing the selflessness of parenthood and the unconditional love demonstrated by Christ, you can build a foundation of love that is resilient, fulfilling, and built to last.

Loving Through Imperfections

You might be thinking, *You don't get it. They have so many flaws, and I really don't like them right now. They just irk me.* It's a natural feeling, but here's the truth: we're all flawed. No one is immune to mistakes, and every day brings an opportunity to grow. Relationships aren't about finding someone perfect—they're about choosing someone you can love even when they're imperfect. Love isn't just about who you can live with; it's about who you *can't live without.*

If you've chosen someone to build a life with, it means the positives outweigh the negatives. But in moments of frustration, it's easy to lose sight of that. When this happens, remind yourself of why you fell in love with them. Write down the qualities that drew you to them—their kindness, their humor, their resilience. Reflecting on these traits can reignite feelings of gratitude and connection.

Remember the *4 Ps*—Patience, Persistence, Protection, and Progress. These principles help you shift your focus from frustration to growth, allowing you to see how far you've come together. They also remind you that your partner is by your side, loving you through your own imperfections. Relationships are about mutual effort and grace. Just as you extend understanding to them, they're doing the same for you.

Few worthwhile things in life come easily. Whether it's going to the gym, eating healthy, or building wealth, each requires effort, commitment, and consistent progression. Relationships are no different—they, too, demand intentional work and a dedication to growth. Ultimately, no relationship is free of struggles, and no person is without flaws. But love is about choosing to grow together, to see the potential in each other, and to build a bond that goes beyond surface frustrations. When you focus on the progress, the partnership, and the love that connects you, those imperfections become opportunities for deeper connection and lasting strength.

Choosing Love Everyday

So choose wisely. Life is a series of endless choices, and every day presents us with the opportunity to choose who we love and how we show that love. When you decide to spend your life with someone, it's not a one-time decision—it's a daily commitment. Love isn't just an emotion; it's an active choice that requires intention and effort.

Love is a privilege, an opportunity that not everyone experiences, and it should be cherished like gold during the California Gold Rush. In the mid-1800s, people uprooted their lives, left behind security, and risked everything in pursuit of what they believed was valuable and life-changing. Similarly, the decision to love someone deeply and fully has the potential to transform your life. If you've chosen the right person, that commitment is a treasure worth every ounce of effort.

By reminding yourself each day that you're actively choosing to love your partner, you reclaim control over your emotions and reactions. This mindset allows little room for prolonged frustration or resentment because you acknowledge that love is your choice—it's a reflection of your values and priorities. Choosing love daily means being intentional about making the most of every moment you share with your partner.

The ultimate goal in a relationship is to ensure your partner feels loved. This can be expressed in countless ways: through kind words, acts of service, physical affection, or simply being present. Verbal affirmations like, *"I appreciate you"* or *"I'm grateful for everything you do"* can go a long way. Actions, too, speak volumes—taking the time to listen, planning small surprises, or handling a responsibility so they can rest shows your love in meaningful ways.

Loving someone is a gift, both to give and to receive. When you approach your relationship with the same passion and determination as someone chasing gold, you're not only valuing your partner—you're also enriching your life. Treat your love as the treasure it is, and nurture it with intention, gratitude, and purpose every single day.

The Impact

Loving unconditionally transforms the way your partner feels about themselves and your relationship. It makes them feel fully accepted—flaws and all. Knowing they are loved without conditions creates a sense of security, encouraging them to be their authentic self. When your partner feels safe, they're more likely to open up about internal struggles, trusting that you'll stand by them through it all. It's like visiting a good doctor—you're willing to share everything because you know they're there to help, not judge.

UNCONDITIONAL LOVE ISN'T EASY. IT'S POWERFUL.

Unconditional love is also liberating, both for the giver and the receiver. When expectations are tied to love, it can be overwhelming and exhausting. Imagine if your partner expected you to be perfect all the time; the pressure to constantly prove yourself would be draining. As humans, we thrive on positive reinforcement. Focusing on progress instead of shortcomings motivates growth and creates space for personal and relational development.

This type of love mirrors the love Christ has for us: *"But God commendeth his love toward us, in that, while we were yet sinners, Christ died for us."* His love is not based on our worthiness or actions but is freely given, despite our flaws. When we love others unconditionally, we reflect the same grace and mercy that Christ extends to us. By modeling our love after His, we create relationships rooted in patience, forgiveness, and unwavering support.

Ultimately, unconditional love removes the need to "earn" affection and replaces it with the freedom to simply *be loved.* This freedom builds trust, strengthens the bond between partners, and allows both individuals to experience a love that is not only human but also reflects the divine.

"But God commendeth his love toward us, in that, while we were yet sinners, Christ died for us"

How to Implement

It's one thing to talk about it, but it's another thing to do it. These four elements are the cornerstones of lasting connections, creating an environment where love can flourish without the weight of unrealistic expectations or transactional demands.

Acceptance Over Perfection: In parenthood, a child is loved simply for who they are, not for what they accomplish. Similarly, in romantic relationships, love means embracing your partner as they are rather than attempting to mold them into an ideal. This doesn't mean ignoring challenges but instead offering support and understanding through them. Acceptance fosters trust, providing a safe space for both partners to grow together without fear of rejection. Be sure to practice empathy and include daily affirmations to reinforce any progress.

Acts of Selfless Giving: Parenthood often involves endless sacrifices, from sleepless nights to giving up personal time, all without expecting anything in return. The same spirit of selflessness strengthens romantic relationships. Small, thoughtful gestures—like preparing a favorite meal, leaving an encouraging note or simply listening when your partner needs to vent—speak volumes. True giving isn't about reciprocity; it's about valuing and uplifting the other person. Try to be as present as possible. In today's society, it's easy to be lulled away by technology or social media.

Forgiveness as a Default: Both children and partners will make mistakes—this is inevitable. Parents know the importance of grace, forgiving a child who accidentally breaks a cherished item or struggles with disobedience. In romantic relationships, holding onto resentment only builds barriers. Instead, forgiveness acknowledges human imperfection while prioritizing healing and forward movement. Forgiveness is not about excusing every mistake but about choosing to preserve the relationship over holding onto anger. Always try to focus on the bigger picture and remind each other you're both on the same team.

Encouragement and Support: A parent's role as a cheerleader for their child mirrors the support required in romantic love. Just as a parent celebrates a child's successes and comforts them through failures, partners should do the same for each other. Whether it's standing by during a career change or supporting personal growth, encouragement builds confidence and reinforces the partnership. Loving freely means prioritizing your partner's well-being and growth, even when it takes effort or sacrifice. Continue to be their safe space.

DIRTY DIAPERS

EMBRACING HUMILITY IN LOVE AND SERVICE

2,325. That's the average number of diapers a parent changes in a year when they have a baby, according to the American Academy of Pediatrics. That's 2,325 moments when a parent or guardian swallows their ego, pride, and personal preferences to care for another human being in one of the least glamorous ways possible. Few people—if any—are lining up to voluntarily change diapers without some form of compensation. Yet, parents willingly and consistently take on this task without hesitation, driven by love, responsibility, and an unshakable desire to care for their child. It's a vivid and humbling reminder of the power of love in action.

Think about it: no parent gets excited to clean up a smelly, messy diaper. It's inconvenient, unpleasant, and sometimes downright revolting. And yet, when the time comes, parents don't just delay the task indefinitely. They step up, not because they enjoy it but because their child's well-being takes priority over their comfort. This willingness to lower oneself, to set aside personal pride, is a clear demonstration of humility. Even if the child's diaper is the worst they've ever seen (or smelled), the parent will eventually take the initiative to clean it up—not because they feel like it, but because they understand that love requires action.

This same relentlessness in humility is essential for the person you choose to spend your life with. While diaper duty may seem far removed from adult relationships, the principle of humility at its core is universal. A parent changing diapers exemplifies **freedom from pride or arrogance**, which is the very definition of humility. It's the understanding that love means putting someone else's needs above your own—even when it's inconvenient, uncomfortable, or unpleasant.

Humility in Action

Have you ever been in a disagreement with your partner, knowing they were wrong, yet they refused to let it go? Most of us have experienced this at some point. Sometimes, the tension escalates to the point where both of you are upset, and taking time apart to cool off feels like the only option. In those moments, have you ever thought to yourself, *"I'm not going to talk to them. They can come to me—I'm right!"* If so, you're human. But I'm here to tell you, most times, this isn't the best approach.

When emotions are stripped away, determining who's right or wrong often isn't the most important factor. In relationships, the goal should be to succeed together as a team. If you're on the same team, one person can't win while the other loses. If one of you is losing, the relationship as a whole suffers. It's both of you against the problem, not one against the other. With this perspective, reconciliation becomes the ultimate goal.

There's nothing wrong with taking time to gather your thoughts or cool down when emotions are running high. In fact, this can prevent unnecessary escalation. However, allowing pride or ego to create a wedge between you and your partner is counterproductive. The more humility you bring to the table, the more approachable and understanding you become. Humility fosters openness and trust, making it easier for your partner to feel they can talk to you about anything.

I remember an experience in college that taught me the value of humility in relationships and communication. I had a professor who made students feel small every time they tried to answer his questions in class. He seemed more interested in asserting his dominance than fostering learning.

Unsurprisingly, the class was miserable, and I barely remember anything he taught. In contrast, I had a finance professor who taught us about the stock market through a portfolio-building competition. One day, he openly shared his past mistakes and bad investments, using them as lessons for us. His vulnerability and humility created an incredible environment where everyone felt engaged and willing to learn. That class remains one of my most memorable because he led with humility rather than ego.

Humility is a powerful thing. As parents, for example, we often put someone else's needs before our own. That act of prioritizing another person sends a profound message: *"They matter more than my pride or momentary frustrations."* This mindset is freeing because it reveals a larger purpose—one rooted in love, growth, and shared success. Sometimes, you must be the change you wish to see. By leading with humility, openness, and a willingness to reconcile, you set the tone for a relationship built on mutual respect and understanding.

Let me guess—you hesitate to show humility because you think it might come off as a sign of weakness. I've heard many men express concerns that if they show vulnerability, their partners won't respect them or treat them as they'd like. But here's the hard truth: if you let someone else dictate your behavior or hold you back from doing what's right, *that* is a true weakness. Strength comes from the courage to rise above the norm and stand out from the crowd.

HUMILITY ISN'T WEAKNESS—IT'S STRENGTH UNDER CONTROL.

True leaders don't rely on force to command respect. Instead, they inspire others through their vision, purpose, and actions. Consider Gandhi, who was revered for his philosophy of nonviolence. Time and again, he demonstrated humility, using peaceful resistance to unite people and effect change. Similarly, Nelson Mandela became a symbol of unity and reconciliation, emphasizing forgiveness even when retaliation seemed justified. He understood that there was a greater purpose at stake. Mother Teresa dedicated her life to serving the poor and the sick, and her unwavering compassion inspired countless others to follow in her footsteps.

Just as children look to their parents and mimic their behaviors, our partners often reflect the energy and example we set. Your circle shapes who you become, so why not lead by example and influence your partner in a positive way? True strength lies in inspiring those around you, not through dominance but through integrity, humility, and purpose.

Time to Serve

Serving your partner. What exactly does that mean? It means prioritizing their needs and honoring them. It seems simple, right? But in practice, it requires intentional effort, selflessness, and a willingness to put their well-being at the forefront of your actions consistently. We all have a lot going on, but paying attention to the details matters. Think about having a newborn baby. They can't use words to communicate, so you have to pay attention to every little cue. Each cry means something different, and it typically becomes a process of elimination: are they hungry, do they need a diaper change, or are they sleepy? Over time, many parents develop an instinct and can tell what their baby needs just by observing them.

As children grow, you still have to pay attention to their cues, but they begin to communicate more clearly. The same principle applies to your partner. Early in a relationship, you might not immediately know what they need, but over time, if you're attentive, it becomes easier to recognize their cues. Spending time truly getting to know your partner is key to serving them in a way that makes them feel loved.

If you're unsure where to start, understanding their love language is a great first step. For example, if your partner's love language is receiving gifts, you can find opportunities to show love in that way. Let's say she's had a tough week at work. Sending her a bouquet of flowers to her job with a note that says, *"Just like these flowers, you bring beauty and light to the world—even during tough weeks. Here's a little reminder of how amazing you are. Take a deep breath, relax, and let yourself bloom again. You've got this!"* shows that you're paying attention to what's going on in her life while also speaking her love language.

On the other hand, if her love language is acts of service, you might greet her after work with a foot spa ready. Pampering her with a foot soak and massage is a thoughtful way to show love. Some men hesitate to do things like washing someone's feet, but self-sacrifice is life-changing. If you think acts of service like this are beneath you, consider the example set by Christ, who humbly washed His disciples' feet. Even though they felt unworthy, He did it anyway, demonstrating humility and love. This is the kind of mindset we should aim to embody in our relationships.

Every day, we should seek new ways to serve our partner and improve their lives. Imagine the peace you'd feel knowing your partner was doing everything possible to improve your life. When both people in a relationship adopt this selfless approach, it builds trust, love, and an unshakeable foundation. True service isn't about grand gestures but about consistently showing up with humility, love, and intentionality.

Sometimes We're Wrong

In relationships, humility often means acknowledging that we're not always right. While this might feel uncomfortable, being willing to admit when we're wrong is one of the most important ways we can build trust, respect, and intimacy with our partners. It requires self-reflection, vulnerability, and a genuine desire to grow—not just for our own sake but for the sake of the relationship.

Let's look at 2 examples:

First off, imagine promising your child you'll help them with their homework after dinner, but then you get caught up in a work email and miss the opportunity. When your child expresses disappointment, the easiest response is to brush it off with, *"I had important work to do."* But what message does that send? It teaches them that your commitments to them are flexible or less important than other priorities. Secondly, you've had a long week at work and decide to unwind by going out with friends on a Friday night. You assure your partner you won't be out late, but the good times roll on, and before you know it, it's midnight. Your partner was expecting you home earlier, possibly to spend some quality time or to share the responsibilities of winding down the day with the kids. By the time you get home, they're upset—not just because you were late, but because they feel undervalued.

It's easy to get defensive in moments like these. You might think, *"I deserve to have some fun after a hard week,"* or *"It's not a big deal—I'm here now, aren't I?"* But humility calls for a different approach. Instead of deflecting blame or minimizing their feelings, this is an opportunity to practice self-reflection and take responsibility for your actions.

Start by acknowledging the mistake. For example, you could say: *"I realize I stayed out later than I said I would, and I understand that it upset you. That wasn't fair to you, and I'm sorry."* This simple acknowledgment does two important things: it validates your partner's feelings and shows that you're taking ownership of your actions.

Next, express your willingness to address the issue and improve. This might look like saying: *"I didn't prioritize our time together tonight, and I see how that affected you. I'll make sure this doesn't happen again. In the future, I'll set clearer boundaries for myself when I go out, and I'll check in with you if plans change."* Communicating your plan for improvement shows that you're not just apologizing to smooth things over but are genuinely committed to growth.

Part of this process involves considering your partner's perspective and advice. Maybe your partner has expressed in the past that they feel left out or unimportant when you prioritize social time over family time. Instead of brushing off their concerns or assuming you know best, approach the situation with humility: *"I'd like to hear your thoughts on how I can balance my time better. I want to make sure you feel valued and supported."* This willingness to learn from your partner demonstrates that you value their input and recognize that you don't always have all the answers.

Humility also means recognizing that your partner's opinions and insights can be valuable in other areas of life. No one is the smartest person in the room on every topic, and relationships thrive when both people respect and learn from each other's strengths. For example, if your partner suggests ways to manage your time better or offers insight into why certain actions upset them, take their advice seriously. Instead of defaulting to defensiveness or dismissing their input, reflect on it. You might realize that their perspective helps you see blind spots you hadn't considered. This openness to feedback and self-improvement fosters a relationship dynamic rooted in respect and growth. By admitting when you're wrong, you create a safe space where both partners can communicate honestly without fear of judgment. It also models humility and encourages your partner to approach conflicts with the same mindset.

Finally, follow through on your commitment to change. Words alone are not enough; your actions must reflect your intentions. If you've promised to prioritize family time, make an effort to plan a special evening together or ensure that your social outings don't interfere with your commitments at home. Small, consistent actions show that you take your partner's feelings seriously and are actively working to improve.

At its core, admitting when we're wrong is about placing the relationship above our ego. It's a way of saying, *"I care more about us than about being right."* This kind of humility strengthens the bond between partners and allows both people to grow individually and together. It reminds us that relationships are not about perfection but about effort, self-awareness, and a shared commitment to making each other's lives better. In every relationship, there will be times when we fall short. What matters most is how we respond to those moments. By owning our mistakes, reflecting on how we can do better, and valuing our partner's input, we show that we're invested in the relationship and in becoming the best version of ourselves. That's what builds a lasting connection.

Making Humility a Habit

Humility isn't confined to grand, self-sacrificing moments—it's often found in the daily, seemingly small acts of care and consideration we offer to those we love. It's the parent who changes their baby's diaper for the 2,325th time that year without expecting recognition or gratitude. It's the spouse who puts down their phone to truly listen when their partner speaks. These small choices reveal the quiet strength of humility, where love takes precedence over pride, convenience, or ego.

Consider a newborn's needs. They don't understand where their food comes from or what it takes to provide it—they simply know they're hungry and expect to be fed. When our son wakes in the middle of the night, half-asleep and crying softly at first, he's not concerned with how tired we are or the effort it takes to warm a bottle. If the minutes pass and his hunger isn't met, his cries grow louder, but once he's fed, he drifts back to sleep, blissfully unaware of the work involved. There's no "thank you," no pat on the back, no acknowledgment at all. And yet, as parents, we don't expect it. We know it's our responsibility to provide what he needs, no matter how inconvenient or exhausting it might be.

This kind of selflessness is a daily demonstration of humility. It's about placing someone else's well-being above your own, not for recognition, but because it's the right thing to do. The same servant-hearted mindset applies to our relationships with partners. Just as a parent prioritizes their child's needs without hesitation, we must approach our relationships with the same relentlessness in humility.

In daily life with a partner, humility is found in the quiet choices that build trust and connection over time. It's taking a moment to listen without interrupting when your partner is sharing their thoughts, even if you've had a long day yourself. It's choosing to ask, *"How can I help lighten your load today?"* instead of waiting for them to ask. These gestures might seem small, but they send a powerful message: *"Your needs and feelings matter to me."*

Daily humility also shows up in how we handle conflicts. When disagreements arise, humility allows us to pause and consider our partner's perspective instead of rushing to defend our own. It's admitting, *"I may have misunderstood,"* or, *"You're right, I didn't think about it that way,"* even when it's hard. These moments of vulnerability and accountability are not signs of weakness but of strength, reinforcing the idea that the relationship is a partnership, not a competition.

Humility impacts how we express appreciation. It's easy to assume our partner knows we're grateful for their efforts, but humility reminds us to vocalize it: *"Thank you for handling dinner tonight—I know you've had a busy day too."* These acknowledgments may seem small, but they create an environment of mutual respect and recognition where both partners feel seen and valued.

It's also reflected in how we handle the mundane responsibilities of life. Folding laundry, cleaning up after dinner, or taking care of errands without expecting praise are acts of service that speak volumes. These tasks might go unnoticed, but when done with a humble heart, they contribute to a sense of shared partnership and love. They say, *"I'm here for you, not because I have to be, but because I want to be."*

Humility in a relationship also means letting go of the need to always be right. It's choosing to focus on the bigger picture—building a loving, supportive bond—rather than proving a point. It's about putting the relationship above your ego and being willing to compromise, not as a sign of defeat but as an act of love.

The impact of daily humility on a partnership is profound. It creates an environment where both individuals feel safe, respected, and valued. It fosters open communication, trust, and a shared sense of purpose. By consistently showing up with humility, you lay the foundation for a relationship that can weather challenges, celebrate victories, and grow stronger over time. Humility isn't just about what you do for your partner—it's about how you show up in the relationship every single day. It's the quiet, consistent choice to love selflessly, honor each other's needs, and build a bond rooted in mutual respect and care.

Reflection Time: The Messy Moments Test

Love isn't proven when things are clean. It's proven in the mess. Humility steps up, even when no one's watching. Are you showing up to serve... or waiting to be seen?

- When was the last time you cleaned up a "mess" in your relationship without needing credit?

- Can you think of a time your ego delayed healing when humility could've fixed it sooner?

- What's one "dirty diaper" moment you're avoiding today—and how could choosing humility change the outcome?

BUILT TO PROTECT

EMBRACING PROTECTION AS A SACRED DUTY

I f you're a parent, you know from the moment a child is born there's nothing you won't do to ensure their safety. From the soft spot on their head after birth to their first fall to standing up for them against bullies at school, your primary focus is their well-being. This sense of security you provide allows the child to be carefree, trusting that their parent will protect them from harm. Similarly, in romantic relationships, women seek that same sense of security from their partner. They want someone who can protect them physically, emotionally, financially, and spiritually. Let's explore these dimensions of protection.

Physical Protection

The Bible provides examples of God's protection, such as in Psalm 91:4: "He will cover you with his feathers, and under his wings, you will find refuge; his faithfulness will be your shield and rampart." In relationships, physical protection builds trust and deepens bonds. Beyond responding to threats, being proactive—like maintaining a safe environment and respecting boundaries—demonstrates attentiveness and care.

Proactive physical protection also involves understanding your partner's specific needs and fears. For example, if your partner feels uneasy walking in certain areas at night, offering to accompany them or arranging safe transportation shows that you're attentive to their concerns. It also includes everyday gestures, like checking that their car is in good working condition or ensuring their home is secure with proper locks and alarms. These actions may seem small but convey a significant message: their safety is your priority.

Physical protection also encompasses respecting personal boundaries and ensuring your physical presence is a source of comfort, not intimidation. This means being conscious of body language, tone, and proximity during discussions or disagreements. Protecting your partner isn't just about external threats; it's about making sure your relationship itself feels like a safe haven. Consistency in these actions fosters trust and reassures your partner of your unwavering commitment to their well-being.

Emotional Protection

Emotional protection involves creating a nurturing environment where your partner feels valued and understood. This starts with being emotionally available and actively listening. For example, if your partner struggles with an addiction, your role is to provide a judgment-free space where they feel safe to share. Reinforce their worth by reminding them they are more than their struggles.

Establishing a recurring time for open discussions, where one partner listens without judgment, helps foster emotional safety. Controlling your expressions and focusing on their needs shows prioritization of their well-being. Ephesians 4:2 advises, "Be completely humble and gentle; be patient, bearing with one another in love." Patience, humility, and gentleness create a secure foundation for emotional protection.

Emotional protection also means understanding and validating your partner's feelings, even when you may not fully agree. This requires empathy and the willingness to see situations from their perspective. For instance, if your partner is overwhelmed by work stress, responding with understanding and offering practical support, like helping with household responsibilities, demonstrates your care.

REAL LOVE WHISPERS, "YOU'RE SAFE HERE."

It's equally important to set aside intentional time for your partner. In today's fast-paced world, distractions are everywhere. By prioritizing uninterrupted moments to connect, you reaffirm their significance in your life. This might be as simple as a weekly date night, a morning coffee chat, or a daily check-in where you focus solely on each other. Such practices build emotional intimacy and reinforce the idea that your relationship is a priority.

Encouraging your partner to express themselves freely, whether about their dreams, fears, or frustrations, is another vital component of emotional protection. Creating this safe space for communication ensures they feel heard and supported, which strengthens the bond and trust in your relationship. Emotional protection, at its core, is about consistently showing your partner that their heart is safe with you.

Financial Protection

Financial stability ensures your partner feels confident in your ability to support each other through challenges. For instance, if either partner faces unemployment, financial protection means reassurance and teamwork to regain stability. Setting financial goals and maintaining transparency builds trust and demonstrates long-term thinking.

Proverbs 21:5 states, "The plans of the diligent lead surely to abundance, but everyone who is hasty comes only to poverty." Responsible planning and consistent actions create a secure foundation. Budgeting, maintaining an emergency fund, and working together to manage resources are key steps in fostering financial protection.

Financial protection also involves honest communication about money. Being transparent about your financial situation, goals, and concerns helps build trust and align priorities. If one partner tends to handle finances, regular check-ins can ensure both are aware and involved in decision-making, fostering a sense of partnership.

Another critical aspect is supporting each other during financial challenges. For example, if one partner loses a job or faces unexpected expenses, the other can step in to share the burden, providing both practical help and emotional encouragement. This sense of teamwork not only alleviates stress but also strengthens the relationship.

Long-term financial protection includes planning for the future together. This might involve saving for significant milestones like buying a home, funding education, or preparing for retirement. Sharing and working toward these goals creates a sense of security and reinforces your commitment to building a stable future together. Financial protection, ultimately, is about demonstrating reliability and ensuring your partner feels secure in your shared journey.

Spiritual Protection

Spiritual protection is about setting a strong foundation through prayer, scripture, and worship. 1 Thessalonians 5:17 (KJV) encourages, "Pray without ceasing." Praying together and seeking God's guidance fosters unity. Worshiping together, whether attending church or engaging in acts of service, deepens your bond and keeps Christ at the center of your relationship.

Practicing biblical principles like forgiveness or gratitude strengthens your spiritual connection. Proverbs 27:17 reminds us, "Iron sharpeneth iron; so a man sharpeneth the countenance of his friend." Spiritual growth is a shared journey that benefits both individuals and the partnership.

Regular spiritual practices create an atmosphere where faith thrives. Setting aside time to read the Bible, discuss its teachings, and reflect on how they apply to your relationship helps keep both partners grounded. Additionally, encouraging each other in personal spiritual growth ensures that faith remains a central pillar of the relationship.

Spiritual protection also involves leading by example. When one partner demonstrates a strong commitment to their faith, it inspires the other to deepen their spiritual journey. This might include volunteering together, participating in church activities, or mentoring others in faith. Such shared experiences not only strengthen your spiritual bond but also reinforce the values that guide your relationship.

Incorporating spiritual protection means being intentional about addressing challenges with prayer and seeking wisdom from God. When disagreements arise, turning to scripture or praying together fosters resolution and unity. Keeping Christ at the center of your relationship ensures that love, forgiveness, and grace are ever-present, providing a solid foundation for enduring partnership.

Built to Protect

Protection is more than instinct—it's a calling. In relationships, protecting your partner reflects God's love and care for His people. Whether physical, emotional, financial, or spiritual, each form of protection says, "I see you, I value you, and I will do my part to ensure your well-being." Like a parent provides safety for their child, partners are called to create an environment where love, trust, and security flourish.

Bible Time

Who: Joseph
What: Emotional, Reputational, and Physical Protection
Where: Matthew 1:19 & Matthew 2:14 (KJV)

Joseph's example of protection is layered and profound. When he discovered Mary was pregnant, rather than reacting impulsively or publicly shaming her, *"being a just man, and not willing to make her a publick example, was minded to put her away privily"* (Matthew 1:19). That was **emotional** and **reputational protection**—he guarded her dignity even before receiving divine confirmation.

But Joseph's role didn't stop there. When warned in a dream that Herod sought to kill the child, he immediately took Mary and Jesus and *"departed into Egypt"* to keep them safe (Matthew 2:14). That was **physical protection**—swift, sacrificial, and brave.

At all turns and opportunities to choose self, Joseph chose to protect his partner and family at all costs. Leaving all he knew, and any expectations he may have had.

He didn't do it for applause. He didn't post about it. He didn't complain. He simply obeyed, and through that obedience, he became a covering—emotionally, physically, and spiritually—for the mother of the Messiah.

Joseph's protection wasn't loud—but it was loyal. And it saved lives.

LOVE MADE VISIBLE

TRANSLATING LOVE INTO ACTION

I f you've found someone that you want to spend the rest of your life with, you've probably said the infamous three words: "I love you." These words form the cornerstone of enduring relationships. However, the ways in which people wish to experience those three words can differ vastly. This is where the concept of love languages, as introduced by Gary Chapman in his book *The 5 Love Languages*, comes into play.

Chapman's idea of love languages reveals that people express and perceive love in unique ways. Much like a parent learning how best to nurture their child—some needing words of encouragement, others thriving with hugs or quality time—partners in romantic relationships must understand how to effectively communicate their love in ways their significant other truly feels.

The 5 Love Languages in Practice

Love languages represent five primary ways people give and receive love: words of affirmation, acts of service, receiving gifts, quality time, and physical touch. These concepts are equally applicable to parenting and romantic relationships, as both require thoughtful attention to how love is conveyed and received.

- **Words of Affirmation**: Verbal expressions such as compliments, encouragement, or gratitude can mean everything. A partner saying, "You're so thoughtful for organizing that dinner with our friends," can make someone feel appreciated and seen. Words of affirmation uplift and validate, strengthening the emotional connection in a relationship.

- **Acts of Service**: Actions that demonstrate care and dedication, such as preparing dinner after a long day, can deeply resonate. For example, a partner might feel truly loved when you take their car to be cleaned or surprise them by finishing a household task they've been dreading. These gestures show love by lightening the load or making life easier.

- **Receiving Gifts**: Often misunderstood as materialistic, this language focuses on the thought and effort behind the gesture. Gifting a partner a meaningful keepsake, such as a photo album of shared memories, or surprising them with their favorite dessert, reminds them of their importance and thoughtfulness.

- **Quality Time**: Undivided attention and shared experiences strengthen bonds. Spending an evening together without distractions, planning a weekend getaway, or taking a walk to discuss your day creates moments of intimacy and connection. These interactions help build lasting memories and reinforce the value of your time together.

- **Physical Touch**: A hug after a long day, holding hands while walking, or cuddling on the couch communicates love and reassurance for those who value this language most. Physical touch fosters intimacy and connection, providing comfort and a sense of security in the relationship.

Translating Love into the Right Language

Understanding your partner's or child's love language is akin to learning their unique dialect. While your expression of love may be sincere, it might not resonate if it doesn't align with how they perceive love. A partner whose love language is acts of service may feel deeply valued when you take on household chores, much like a child appreciates a parent's help with a challenging task. On the other hand, someone who values quality time might not fully register your love if you're distracted during shared moments, just as a child might feel overlooked if a parent isn't fully engaged during playtime.

LOVE ISN'T WHAT YOU SAY. IT'S WHAT THEY FEEL.

Learning a parent's love language can be a deeply rewarding way to strengthen familial bonds. First and foremost, ask them directly how they prefer to receive love. Sometimes, the easiest way to find out is simply to ask, though this approach is often overlooked. For example, you might say, "What makes you feel most appreciated?" or "What can I do to show you how much you mean to me?" These questions open a door for honest conversations about their emotional needs.

Next, observe how they show love to others. Most people tend to express love in ways they themselves like to receive it. A parent who constantly offers to help with tasks might value acts of service, while one who plans family outings may cherish quality time. This observational approach can provide invaluable clues about their love language, even if they aren't consciously aware of it themselves.

Finally, ask for specific examples of times when they felt most loved and appreciated. This could be as simple as, "Can you tell me about a time when someone did something for you that made you feel really special?" These conversations not only provide insight but also deepen the emotional connection between you and your parent. Sharing these stories fosters mutual understanding and creates opportunities to replicate those meaningful gestures.

Recognizing these differences and tailoring your approach ensures that your gestures of love are both understood and appreciated. It's about translating your emotions into a language that your partner, child, or parent comprehends, strengthening the bond and fostering mutual understanding.

Receiving Love

Expressing and receiving love are equally vital in any relationship. You want your partner to appreciate the effort you put into showing love in your own way, just as you aim to do the same for them. For instance, you might spend time finding a thoughtful gift, only for your partner to feel upset because you didn't do the dishes. In such cases, it's important for both of you to recognize and value each other's gestures, even if they don't align perfectly with expectations.

Being open to receiving love in various forms means acknowledging the intention behind the gesture, even when it's not what you anticipated. This flexibility allows you to embrace your partner's efforts and fosters mutual understanding. Whether it's a compliment, a small gift, an act of service, or a physical touch, these expressions of love carry profound meaning when viewed through an appreciative lens.

This approach benefits both partners equally. For example, when you invest time and energy into finding the perfect gift, it's rewarding to know your partner values the thought behind it. Similarly, when your partner expresses love through an act of service, such as making your morning coffee, recognizing their effort ensures they feel appreciated. The willingness to receive love in different forms enriches the relationship, fostering a cycle of giving and gratitude.

Ultimately, embracing love in its many forms strengthens bonds and creates a mutual understanding where both partners feel valued and connected. Acknowledging these expressions of love not only reinforces appreciation but also encourages continued gestures, ensuring love is consistently felt and reciprocated.

The Rewards of Loving in a Way They Understand

When you love your woman in a way that resonates with her deepest needs, your relationship will transform in ways you never imagined. Think of it like giving a child their favorite toy at playtime—the joy is immediate and heartfelt. When a woman feels truly seen, heard, and loved, she becomes a powerful force in your life. Her confidence grows, and she feels emotionally safe, which inspires her to return that love tenfold.

Women who feel valued often go out of their way to make their partners feel equally cherished. She might take the time to cook your favorite meal, plan a game night with your friends, or give you a foot massage after a long day's work—all because she knows you've taken the time to understand her love language. This kind of emotional investment creates a positive feedback loop. The more you make her feel loved in her way, the more she'll naturally want to love you in ways that resonate with you.

Men often underestimate how impactful it is to make a woman feel emotionally secure. When she knows that you see her, hear her, and prioritize her emotional needs, she will open up to you in ways that create a profound and lasting connection.

THE MORE YOU POUR INTO HER, THE MORE
SHE POURS INTO YOU.

Emotional security makes her feel safe enough to be vulnerable, to express her true self, and to invest fully in the relationship. Moreover, understanding her love language fosters intimacy—both emotional and physical. When she feels loved in her way, she becomes more open to deepening the connection in all areas of the relationship. Physical intimacy becomes more meaningful when it's rooted in emotional understanding. Holding her hand, offering a reassuring hug, or simply being present when she needs you speaks volumes in her love language, which, in turn, strengthens the overall bond. One of the greatest rewards of loving her in a way she understands is the trust it builds. Trust is the foundation of any successful relationship, and when she knows that you've taken the time to learn her emotional needs, her trust in you deepens. She'll know that she can rely on you to be attentive, caring, and present. This trust will make her more comfortable communicating openly and honestly, which is essential for long-term success.

By investing in her emotional well-being, you're not only making her feel loved but also building a partnership that will stand the test of time. Remember, when she feels truly loved, she will become your biggest supporter, your confidante, and your most loyal partner.

Story Time

Jacob was the kind of man who believed love should be shown through action. He took pride in surprising Leslie with lavish gifts—handbags, concert tickets, spontaneous weekend trips. To him, those gestures were the ultimate expression of devotion. But to Leslie, something always felt... missing.

At first, she smiled through it. The gifts were thoughtful, and she was grateful. But deep down, she longed for something more personal—something money couldn't buy. Leslie's love language was words of affirmation. She needed to hear things like, *"I'm proud of you,"* or *"I love how thoughtful you are."* But those words rarely came.

Over time, their relationship hit turbulence. Leslie began to feel emotionally disconnected, even unloved, while Jacob felt confused and unappreciated. *"I do all these things for her,"* he thought, *"and it's like it doesn't matter."*

Eventually, they sat down for a heart-to-heart. Jacob voiced his frustration, and Leslie, through tears, explained that while she appreciated everything he did, what she truly needed was to hear how he felt about her. She wasn't asking for more effort—she just needed it expressed in a different form.

That conversation was a turning point. Once Jacob got past his own perspective and leaned into Leslie's emotional needs, everything changed. He began leaving her notes, sending thoughtful texts, and speaking life over her regularly. Their connection deepened, and as a bonus, he even saved some money in the process.

Moral of the story: The way you *give* or *receive* love may not be the same way your partner needs to receive it. You wouldn't put diesel in a gas-only car—even if diesel works for other vehicles. To love well, you have to know what kind of fuel your relationship actually runs on.

GRACE IN THE GAPS

UNMERITED FAVOR

H ave you ever been in a situation where your significant other keeps making the same mistake over and over again? Depending on the issue, it can be incredibly frustrating. For instance, one of my personal pet peeves is "smacking." If you're unfamiliar with the term, it's the sound people make when chewing food with their mouths open. To some, it might seem trivial, but to me, it's like my ears have been tuned to amplify that sound tenfold. Small things like this can have an outsized impact on our mood and demeanor.

Whatever the issue, these situations can be particularly exasperating when you've communicated how much it bothers you and the behavior persists. By the third or fourth time, it's easy to feel as if your partner doesn't care or is intentionally trying to push your buttons. At that point, you may even think they don't deserve another chance. And honestly? You're probably right—they don't. But here's the key: Grace isn't about what's deserved. It's about **giving unmerited favor**, even when it isn't earned.

Grace is one of the most important foundations of a sustainable relationship. If you've chosen this person as a potential life partner, it's worth reminding yourself why. You've seen value in their best qualities, or you've felt an undeniable connection. You want to build a future with them. And building anything meaningful requires grace because no one is a finished product.

Grace is a byproduct of unconditional love. They may not deserve another chance, but you love them enough to give it anyway. The greatest example of grace is Christ's offer of salvation. Despite our countless shortcomings, God's love paid the price in full through Christ's death, burial, and resurrection. That gift isn't about what we deserve; it's about love that transcends merit.

Why Grace?

Grace isn't optional in a thriving relationship; it's essential. Think of the people in your life who have shown you the most grace. Maybe it's a parent, a mentor, or a friend. What do you feel when you think about them? Likely, they represent a safe space for you—a place where you're accepted despite your flaws. Now, imagine extending that same gift to your partner.

GRACE MAKES SPACE FOR GROWTH.

When you practice grace, you create an environment where your partner feels safe to grow, learn, and even fail. Relationships are not about demanding perfection but about fostering an atmosphere where both individuals can become the best versions of themselves. Without grace, resentment and bitterness can quickly take root, eroding the foundation of your partnership.

Grace also reminds us that we are all flawed. It's easy to focus on our partner's mistakes while overlooking our own. But grace requires humility. It calls us to recognize our imperfections and approach our partner with the same understanding we hope to receive.

Grace vs. Enabling

Some might argue that extending grace repeatedly allows bad behavior to continue. While it's true that grace involves forgiveness, it doesn't mean enabling harmful patterns. Grace must be balanced with healthy boundaries and clear communication. Grace and enabling are often confused, but they are fundamentally different. Grace involves forgiveness and understanding, while enabling allows harmful behaviors to persist unchecked. In relationships, this distinction becomes particularly critical when dealing with significant challenges such as infidelity.

Infidelity is a betrayal of trust that requires careful navigation. Offering grace in such situations doesn't mean ignoring the severity of the behavior or tolerating ongoing harm. Instead, it means approaching the situation with a spirit of forgiveness while setting firm boundaries to ensure accountability and growth within the relationship.

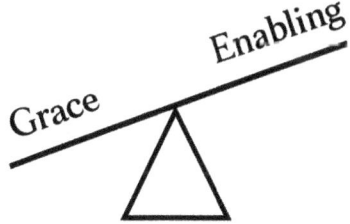

For instance, extending grace to an unfaithful partner might involve working through the pain together, seeking counseling, and rebuilding trust. However, it also requires a commitment from the offending partner to acknowledge their actions and demonstrate consistent change. Without these steps, grace can quickly devolve into enabling, which allows destructive patterns to continue unchecked.

A practical example of grace versus enabling can be seen in parenting. Imagine a child refusing to eat their vegetables. You can extend grace by understanding their dislike and encouraging them gently. However, enabling would mean letting them avoid vegetables entirely, depriving them of essential nutrition and the opportunity to develop healthier habits.

Grace involves patience and persistence while still guiding them toward progress and accountability.

GRACE ISN'T WEAKNESS. IT'S PATIENCE WITH PURPOSE.

Navigating these challenging situations requires a deep understanding of what grace truly means. It's about love and forgiveness, yes, but also about fostering growth, accountability, and mutual respect within the relationship. Enabling, by contrast, undermines these goals and allows destructive patterns to persist. It's also important to remember the 4 Ps—Prayer, Patience, Practice, and Persistence—discussed in the previous chapter. These principles provide a framework for navigating challenges while extending grace.

Steps to Practice Grace Daily

Incorporating grace into your daily life may seem challenging at first, but breaking it down into actionable steps can make it manageable. Here are some ways to integrate grace into your relationship with intention:

Take a Moment to Reflect: When conflicts arise, don't react instantly. Instead, pause and reflect on the situation. What triggered your feelings? What might your partner be experiencing? By giving yourself a moment, you'll gain clarity and avoid reacting impulsively. You'll be less likely to regret your response.

Shift Your Perspective: Put yourself in your partner's shoes. Consider the pressures or challenges they might be experiencing. This shift can help you approach the situation with empathy instead of frustration. Give them the benefit of the doubt.

Use Gentle Words: When discussing an issue, choose words that foster understanding. Speak calmly and kindly, even if you're upset. For instance, instead of saying, "You never listen to me," try, "I feel unheard, and it's important to me that we address this." Compassionate communication opens doors for resolution.

Forgive with Intention: Forgiveness doesn't mean ignoring the hurt or pretending it didn't happen. It means consciously deciding to let go of resentment and work toward healing. Remember, forgiveness benefits both of you by creating space for growth.

Recognize Efforts: Celebrate your partner's small steps to improvement. Whether it's remembering a minor request or making an effort to communicate better, acknowledging their progress builds positivity and encouragement.

Now, not by any means is this always easy. Dealing with issues that happen over and over again can be draining, frustrating, and sometimes even feel overwhelming. Over time, however, implementing these steps makes it easier to progress in consistently giving grace. A helpful way to de-escalate the frustration you may feel is by remembering that each human being has strengths and weaknesses, including your partner.

With that said, some behaviors fall into the "weakness" category and tend to require more grace. For example, if your partner is a poor communicator when they're frustrated, it's unrealistic to expect them to fix it overnight. Progress often comes in small increments, and it's essential to recognize those efforts. Let's say your partner tends to yell and use profanity when upset. Then, during the next argument, they raise their voice but manage to avoid using profanity. While they may still not be at the level of communication you desire, their effort to improve is evident and should be acknowledged.

Offering grace means encouraging these incremental improvements while maintaining patience. By focusing on progress instead of perfection, you create a supportive environment that fosters growth. In time, these small steps can lead to meaningful and lasting change, strengthening your relationship and reinforcing the foundation of unconditional love.

Grace is not about ignoring faults or accepting harmful behavior; it's about fostering an environment of understanding and support that inspires both partners to become better. As you practice grace, you're investing in the long-term health and resilience of your relationship, creating a bond that can withstand challenges and flourish over time.

Bible Time

Who: Jesus Christ
What: Grace
Where: The Cross

The greatest example of grace is found in Jesus Christ's redemptive sacrifice on the cross. Humanity, as a whole, has fallen short and participated in sin. Yet, instead of receiving the full consequences of our actions, we have been offered salvation through grace. This unmerited favor is encapsulated in **Ephesians 2:8: "For by grace are ye saved through faith; and that not of yourselves: it is the gift of God."**

In our imperfections, we deserve judgment and separation from God. However, Christ's sacrifice changed everything. He stood in our place, accepting the penalty for sin on our behalf. This act of grace was not dependent on our worthiness or actions but on God's unconditional love for us. It is the ultimate demonstration of love and forgiveness, providing a path for reconciliation with God.

Imagine the magnitude of this grace. Despite our failures, we are given a chance to start anew, free from the weight of guilt and shame. Grace is not something we can earn through good deeds or merit; it is a divine gift extended to all who believe and have faith in Christ.

Jesus' death and resurrection are more than historical events—they are the foundation of our hope and the ultimate example of how grace operates. His life teaches us to extend grace to others as He did for us. By forgiving those who wronged Him, healing the broken, and showing compassion to the outcast, Christ modeled a grace-filled life.

In understanding this example, we are called to reflect on how we can embody grace in our own lives. Whether it's forgiving a loved one, showing patience to a stranger, or offering compassion to someone in need, extending grace is our way of mirroring Christ's love.

This divine grace is not limited by time or circumstance. It reminds us that no matter how far we've strayed, we are never beyond redemption. Through Christ, we are offered the ultimate gift: salvation and the promise of eternal life.

"And as ye would that men should do to you, do ye also to them likewise."

The Grace Challenge

Take a moment to reflect on your current relationship and identify instances where you could have extended grace but didn't. Consider how your partner might have felt in those moments and how the situation could have been handled differently.

Write down your reflections and share them with your partner as a step toward building a grace-filled relationship. This exercise not only fosters open communication but also helps you internalize the concept of grace and experience its transformative power in your life.

Man in the Mirror

Where Accountability Begins

Your level of commitment, consistency, and integrity should be a reflection of your character, not a reaction to someone else's actions. Our treatment of her should not be contingent upon her actions; rather, it should be a reflection of your integrity and character.

Hindsight is 20/20, But Accountability is 20/10

One of the biggest struggles men face is not realizing the strain they are placing on their relationships until it's too late. It often takes constant nagging, repeated arguments, or even the painful experience of losing the person they truly care about before they recognize their shortcomings.

Hindsight makes things crystal clear— once the relationship has suffered, it's easy to look back and see where you went wrong. But real accountability sharpens your vision **to 20/10**, allowing you to see your flaws before they create irreversible damage. Instead of waiting for your partner to reach their breaking point, take proactive steps to evaluate yourself regularly.

Taking time to look in the mirror periodically and assess how you are showing up in the relationship creates a healthier dynamic. When your partner sees that you consistently strive to be the best version of yourself—not because she forces you to but because you hold yourself to that standard—it fosters trust and emotional security. A woman feels at peace with a man who is self-aware and committed to growth.

A King's Mindset

Throughout history, kings have been held to a higher standard. They could not afford to let personal grievances or the attitudes of their subjects dictate their leadership. A great king understood that his duty to his people was independent of whether they always appreciated or respected him. Leading by example is a crucial aspect of leadership. You cannot expect your partner to be accountable if you fail to demonstrate accountability yourself. Imagine being frustrated with your partner for leaving dishes in the sink instead of washing them, yet for the past week, you have been doing the same. How receptive do you think they will be to your criticism? However, if you have consistently modeled the behaviors and actions you expect, they are more likely to follow suit. Effective leadership in a relationship is about embodying the standards you wish to see in your partner.

Consider King David from the Bible. He was far from a perfect man, but he always took responsibility for his actions. When he failed, he repented. When he made mistakes, he acknowledged them before God and his people. His greatness was not in being flawless but in being accountable.

A king cannot rule effectively if he blames his subjects for his shortcomings. Likewise, a man cannot lead his relationship effectively if he constantly points fingers at his partner instead of working on himself. If your words cause harm, own up to it. If your actions create distance, address it. If you have fallen short, correct it. That is the mark of a man worthy of leadership.

The Kid's Way

Think about the way a responsible father operates. A father does not base his love and provision on whether his children 'deserve' it. A child may misbehave, but a good father still provides, teaches, and guides. He does not stop paying the bills, providing food, or protecting them just because they made a mistake. If a father were to suddenly abandon these responsibilities, his child's perception of him would drastically change. The child would begin to feel uncertain, insecure, and perhaps even unloved. Over time, trust would erode, and the child might either rebel or withdraw emotionally, struggling with feelings of neglect or inconsistency. Children learn stability and security from the consistency of their parent's actions, and when a father ceases to uphold his role, the foundation of that relationship begins to crack.

Likewise, a man's consistency should never hinge on his partner's behavior. If you are committed to being an exceptional partner, that commitment should be unwavering. Just as a good father disciplines with love and corrects, a man in a relationship must uphold his standards regardless of external circumstances. Leadership in a relationship is not about reacting to your partner's behavior but about consistently setting a foundation of accountability, growth, and emotional stability.

Just as a child's perception of their father shifts when he ceases to fulfill his responsibilities, a partner's perception of their significant other can change when consistency and effort decline. If a man once prioritized growth, self-improvement, and accountability but then becomes complacent, his partner may start to question his commitment and reliability. Trust begins to erode when words and actions are no longer aligned. However, when a man continuously works to improve himself, it becomes much easier to navigate conflicts and challenges within the relationship. A partner who sees consistent effort and genuine accountability will feel more secure and willing to work through difficulties, knowing that they are with someone who values progress and integrity.

DON'T BLAME THE MIRROR. FIX THE MAN IN IT!

A man who demonstrates accountability through his actions fosters an environment where his partner feels valued and secure. She will recognize that she is with someone who does not shift blame or wait for others to change first but rather takes the initiative to lead by example. This level of consistency creates trust, respect, and a deeper emotional connection between partners.

If your words cause pain, take responsibility and apologize. If your actions fall short, correct them. If you are not making her feel valued, address it. You are the architect of your relationship's environment. It is on you to create an atmosphere of security, love, and trust. With patience, a man in a relationship must communicate and lead with accountability.

The Garden of Eden

The Bible clearly demonstrates that accountability is a fundamental principle for men. One of the strongest examples is found in Adam's response to God in the Garden of Eden. When confronted about eating the forbidden fruit, Adam deflected and blamed Eve: "The woman whom thou gavest to be with me, she gave me of the tree, and I did eat" (Genesis 3:12, KJV). Instead of taking ownership of his mistake, he shifted responsibility.

This moment serves as a reminder that in every situation, a man can find ways to take accountability and improve his approach. Regardless of circumstances, there is always an opportunity for self-reflection and growth. Instead of focusing on external factors or placing blame, a man should examine how his choices, mindset, and responses contributed to the outcome. Whether in personal relationships, career challenges, or leadership roles, true accountability means consistently asking, "What could I have done differently? How can I improve?"

Adam had the opportunity to accept responsibility and seek correction, but instead, he chose to deflect. This pattern of behavior can be seen in modern relationships when men fail to acknowledge their role in conflicts or difficulties. However, a man who embraces accountability strengthens his character and builds trust with those around him. When a man commits to personal growth, he transforms obstacles into lessons and challenges into stepping stones for improvement.

Contrast this with Jesus Christ, the ultimate example of accountability. He took responsibility for the sins of mankind, though He was blameless. He didn't say, "They don't deserve My sacrifice." Instead, He willingly took on suffering because He was committed to His purpose. As stated in Isaiah 53:5 (KJV), "But he was wounded for our transgressions, he was bruised for our iniquities: the chastisement of our peace was upon him; and with his stripes we are healed." That is the highest level of manhood—**accountability, even when it isn't convenient**.

If you desire to be a man of value, your words, actions, and presence must reflect that regardless of how others behave. True leadership is holding yourself to a standard even when no one is watching or appreciating it.

Where Accountability Starts

Accountability is the bedrock of a strong and lasting relationship. When a man takes ownership of his words, actions, and growth, he creates an environment of trust and respect. This responsibility extends beyond reacting to challenges—it requires a proactive approach to self-improvement. A man who consistently holds himself accountable does not wait for problems to arise; he actively works to be the best version of himself, ensuring that his relationship thrives even in difficult moments. Below are key areas where every man must take full responsibility to foster a healthy and fulfilling partnership:

1. **Your Words** – Words have the power to build or destroy. Speak with intention and integrity.

2. **Your Actions** – Every decision, from how you handle conflict to how you express love, matters.

3. **How You Make Your Partner Feel** – It is not just about what you do but how your actions impact her.

4. **Your Growth** – Are you improving as a man, or are you stagnant? Never stop developing yourself.

5. **Your Leadership** – A man leads with love, wisdom, and strength. This does not mean domination but guidance and consistency.

Recap

A great relationship is built on the foundation of accountability. If you want to be the kind of man who commands respect and love, you must first master yourself. Like a player in NBA 2K, you must recognize your weaknesses and improve them. Like a king, you must lead with integrity. Like a father, you must provide stability regardless of external factors. And like Christ, you must hold yourself to a standard of excellence independent of the actions of others.

Being accountable in a relationship is not about being perfect—it's about being responsible. It is about standing firm in your values and showing up for your partner consistently. It is about making sure that when you look in the mirror, you see a man worthy of admiration, not just from others but from yourself.

So, the next time you feel tempted to say, "I'm not doing this because she doesn't deserve it," ask yourself—are you being the man you claim to be? Because true greatness, true manhood, is never contingent on anyone else's actions. It is a personal decision to always operate at your highest level, regardless of the circumstances. That is the mindset of a king. That is the mark of a real man.

"Everyone wants to be great, until it's
time to do what greatness requires."
Chop Wood Carry Water

No Complaints

Drowning Out the Noise

L et's start with the obvious: complaining kills the vibe. It's like background noise that drains energy from a room. But what exactly is **complaining**? It's the repeated expression of dissatisfaction without actively seeking solutions—venting frustration in a way that focuses on problems rather than resolving them. Complaining doesn't solve anything—it just magnifies the issue. It turns molehills into mountains and stretches tension into resentment. Negative situations grow in size and importance when all we do is talk about how bad they are.

Think of complaining like quicksand: the more you struggle and focus on what's wrong, the deeper you sink. You don't escape the problem—you get consumed by it. But when you take action, even small steps toward a solution, the situation starts to shrink. You reclaim control and shift your mindset from helplessness to empowerment.

COMPLAINING IS LIKE QUICKSAND: THE MORE YOU FOCUS ON WHAT'S WRONG, THE DEEPER YOU SINK.

How to Avoid Complaining

The key to avoiding complaining is training your mind to shift focus. When things go wrong (and they will), resist the urge to dwell on the problem. Instead, redirect your energy toward what you can control. There is always something productive you can do, even if it is simply adjusting your mindset.

Focus on the positives in every situation, no matter how small. Gratitude and problem-solving work hand in hand. When you choose to look for solutions instead of sitting in frustration, you not only feel more empowered but also become more enjoyable to be around. That shift in energy helps you and your relationship thrive.

For example, think about when your baby is not sleeping through the night. It is exhausting, frustrating, and overwhelming. Complaining about it, however, does not help the baby sleep. It only makes the experience feel heavier. Relationships work the same way. If something is off, like your partner not helping around the house or missing emotional cues, voicing concern is healthy. Staying stuck in complaint mode, on the other hand, does not move things forward. Looking for ways to support each other or adjust the routine leads to real change. Complaining only keeps you tired.

If something feels unbalanced in the relationship, such as one partner not contributing to household responsibilities or overlooking emotional needs, it is entirely appropriate to express those concerns. Open communication is essential. However, remaining in a cycle of complaints without a focus on resolution creates stagnation. Forward progress only happens when both partners commit to addressing issues constructively.

Instead of using your energy to repeat frustrations, redirect it toward tangible actions that support long-term improvement. This might mean setting clearer expectations, initiating regular check-ins to improve communication, or offering help in ways your partner responds to. Small, consistent adjustments are often more impactful than repeated criticism. When your focus shifts from what went wrong to how it can go better next time, you create space for growth, not tension.

When It Feels Like You're Doing Everything

I know what you might be thinking. There will be moments when it feels like you're carrying the weight of the relationship. You're making an effort, honoring requests, trying to communicate better, and yet, it seems like your partner can't do the one thing you've asked of them. That frustration is real, and it's valid.

There will be times when the relationship feels imbalanced or overwhelming. These moments happen in every partnership. However, it's important to remember that most situations are not as big as they seem in the moment. When emotions run high, problems feel larger and heavier than they truly are. Time has a way of softening the sharp edges. Instead of reacting emotionally, give yourself space to gain perspective. Pause, breathe, and let things settle before you decide how to respond.

Every relationship has a balance of strengths and weaknesses. No two people are perfectly aligned in every area, and that's okay. The key is recognizing where your partner may still be growing. Think about raising a one-year-old child. Would you expect a toddler to carry in all the groceries by themselves? Of course not. Your natural instinct tells you they aren't capable of that yet, but you also know that one day, they will be. The same instinct applies in relationships.

Giving your partner the space and opportunity to grow into the person they are capable of becoming is a powerful act of love. Growth takes time, and expecting someone to instantly meet your expectations without support or development is unrealistic. Think back to when you learned how to read. You had to master the alphabet before you could spell, and you had to learn to spell before you could read sentences. There are foundational steps to every kind of growth.

CARRY THEM—UNTIL THEY CAN WALK WITH YOU.

Take honest inventory. Have you done everything within your ability to set your partner up for success? If you truly care about someone and envision a life with them, your goal should be to help them win in every area of life. Their growth contributes directly to the strength and success of your relationship.

And if you can genuinely say to yourself that you've done everything you truly could, which is rarely the case because new ideas and approaches are endless, then it is time to shift from complaint to gratitude. Gratitude to the One above for giving you the strength, patience, and emotional capacity to cover for someone else's current shortcomings. That is not a weakness. That is leadership. That is love.

There will be seasons in every relationship when one partner gives far more than they receive. It is not always fifty-fifty, and it is not supposed to be. Sometimes it is eighty-twenty. Sometimes it is one hundred to zero. A successful relationship is not about keeping score. It is about having each other's backs when life gets heavy. True partnership is built on the willingness to pick up the slack when the other person is struggling and trusting that they will do the same when the roles reverse. That mutual, unspoken commitment is the blueprint for long-term connection. That is what builds trust. That is what builds loyalty. That is what builds a bond strong enough for marriage.

Perspective Shrinks the Problem

Not every frustrating moment deserves the weight we give it. Sometimes, what feels urgent or emotionally charged in the moment loses its power once we take a step back.

When the emotion fades, the truth often comes into focus. You remember that one missed moment does not define the relationship. What may have felt like disregard in the moment is often the result of distraction, fatigue, or mental overload. It is rarely a lack of care. High emotional intelligence allows you to recognize this distinction. It gives you the ability to pause, step outside of your own frustration, and consider the situation from your partner's point of view.

That level of perspective is powerful. It allows you to respond with grace instead of criticism. It helps you offer understanding without excusing everything, and it keeps the emotional tone of the relationship from spiraling over minor disappointments. Mature love requires that we evaluate intent, not just outcome. A thoughtful pause can save hours of unnecessary conflict and build a foundation of trust and patience that lasts far longer than a single evening gone off course.

This concept is echoed in parenting as well. The way we frame situations and use our words can shape not only outcomes but the emotional development of those around us. For example, research shows that when parents consistently reinforce positive traits, such as telling a child they are capable, intelligent, or resilient, the child is more likely to internalize and embody those qualities. This is supported by studies on the development of a growth mindset, which emphasize that affirming effort and potential leads to greater perseverance and achievement.

On the other hand, negative labels or repeated criticism can diminish self-belief, limiting a child's view of what they are capable of becoming. The same is true in romantic relationships. Your partner often looks to you for emotional cues, and your words have the power to either affirm their strengths or magnify their insecurities. Research on close relationships shows that when one partner validates and affirms the other's strengths, they actually help shape that person into a more ideal version of themselves, a process known as the **Michelangelo phenomenon**.

Perspective allows you to see your partner not only as they are but as who they are becoming. When you choose to reinforce what is good, strong, or admirable in them, you help them grow into that identity. That mindset transforms how you show up in moments of frustration. Rather than reacting with blame, you respond with belief. You speak to their potential, not just their present behavior. And that choice to see the good, even when it is buried under stress or imperfection, is what strengthens emotional connection and long-term growth.

The Difference Between Growth and Complaints

Not everything that sounds like a complaint is harmful. Sometimes, the real issue lies in *how* something is viewed and expressed. There is a major difference between offering feedback that invites growth and voicing concerns in a way that highlights failure. One moves the relationship forward, while the other keeps it stuck in the past.

Understanding this difference can change how your partner receives your message. When your intention is to build, not blame, your words become a tool for connection instead of conflict. The shift is subtle, but the impact is significant.

One of the most important skills in any relationship is learning how to express your needs in a way that inspires cooperation, not defensiveness. That begins by understanding the distinction between a growth-centered conversation and a complaint-centered one. Below is a breakdown to help you recognize and apply the difference in real-time.

Opportunities for Growth

Future-focused. Solution-oriented. Strengthens connection.

- Focuses on how to improve communication or behavior moving forward

- Highlights potential, not just problems

- Encourages teamwork and shared responsibility

- Aims to deepen understanding, not assign blame

Example: "I think there's an opportunity for us to grow in how we communicate during conflict so that we both feel heard and understood."

Complaints or Criticism

Past-focused. Mistake-oriented. Weakens connection.

- Emphasizes what went wrong without offering a solution

- Often rooted in emotion, not clarity

- Can sound like blame, even if unintended

- May make your partner feel attacked, inadequate, or discouraged

Example: "I don't think you listen when I share my feelings. You never seem to make an effort to understand me, and it's always the same story."

Sometimes, you genuinely do need to correct something, and that's valid. Here's the truth: correction without connection rarely lasts. If your partner feels attacked, they may comply for the moment, but the emotional disconnection will linger.

Before you speak, ask yourself: **Am I trying to correct my partner or connect with them?**

The best correction happens *through connection*, not in place of it. The goal is not to avoid difficult conversations. It is to have them in a way that invites partnership. Try the tips below to turn complaints into growth opportunities:

Instead of: "You never help around the house." **Try saying:** "Can we create a routine that feels more balanced for both of us?"

Instead of: "You never make time for me." **Try saying:** "I really value our quality time. Can we be intentional about planning moments to reconnect during the week?"

Instead of: "You don't care about what I need." **Try saying:** "I want to understand your perspective, and I'd love for you to understand mine too. Can we talk through it?"

These shifts may seem small, but they change the entire tone of the conversation. You go from being adversaries to being teammates, working through the issue side by side.

Bible Time

Who: Joseph
What: A Man Who Endured Without Complaining
Where: Genesis 37:28, 39:21, 40:8, 41:40, 50:20; Galatians 6:9 (KJV)

Joseph is a powerful example of someone who faced extreme trials without complaining. From a young age, he endured hardship that many today might not survive. **But rather than complain, Joseph chose quiet faithfulness.** He was sold into slavery by his own brothers:

> *"...they drew and lifted up Joseph out of the pit, and sold Joseph to the Ishmeelites..."*

Instead of becoming bitter, he faithfully served in Potiphar's house. When falsely accused and imprisoned, he didn't complain—he helped others by interpreting dreams.

> *"But the Lord was with Joseph... and gave him favour in the sight of the keeper of the prison."*

> *"Do not interpretations belong to God? Tell me them, I pray you."*

Eventually, he was promoted to second-in-command in Egypt. In time, he forgave and provided for the same brothers who betrayed him.

"Ye thought evil against me; but God meant it unto good..."

Joseph's story shows us that how things begin is not how they have to end. Sometimes things get worse before they get better — but if you stay the course, you will reap.

"...for in due season we shall reap, if we faint not." — *Galatians 6:9 (KJV)*

Stay faithful, stay thankful, and do it without complaining—your breakthrough may be closer than you think.

LAY THE FIRST BRICK

IT STARTS NOW

Wow, if you've made it this far — congratulations! Seriously, take a second to let that sink in. You've made it through a journey of lessons, insights, and tools that will prepare you to become the kind of man a woman would be proud to marry.

Now, I know that looking at everything all at once might feel a little daunting. You might even be asking yourself, *How am I supposed to master all of this?* But don't panic. Perfection is a goal worth aiming for, but it's not a requirement to start. Mastery doesn't happen overnight. Being a great partner, just like being great at anything else, takes time, effort, and patience. The key is to recognize and appreciate the improvements you make along the way. **The real goal is to enjoy the journey while continually getting better.**

Will Smith once shared a story on *The Oprah Winfrey Show* that beautifully captures this idea. When he was a kid, his father had him and his brother rebuild a wall outside his shop. It was a huge task for two young boys, and at first, it seemed impossible. But his father gave them advice that stuck with him for life: *"Don't try to build a wall. Don't set out to build a wall. You say, 'I'm going to lay this brick as perfectly as a brick can be laid.' You do that every single day. And soon, you'll have a wall."*

That lesson applies here, too. It's a reminder that focusing on small wins will take you further than you could ever imagine. When you commit to laying each "brick" — each act of kindness, patience, communication, and understanding — with care and intention, before you know it, you'll have built something strong and lasting.

ONE BRICK AT A TIME.

Take time to self-reflect often. Look back and remind yourself how far you've come. Growth isn't always obvious in the moment, but when you zoom out, you'll see just how much you've evolved.

Marriage isn't the end of the road; it's the birth of a brand-new journey. You and your partner are about to embark on an adventure that neither of you is fully prepared for — and that's perfectly okay. Just like no one is an expert on day one of parenthood, no one is an expert on day one of marriage either. Over time, you'll learn each other. You'll discover new sides of yourselves and your relationship. **Treat her like your child** — love her with patience, protect her with strength, and lead her with care — and the bond you build will last a lifetime.

My hope for you is simple: that you become a man of strength, patience, humility, and love. A man who leads not with pride but with service. A man who listens just as much as he speaks. A man who owns his mistakes grows from them and always shows up — for himself, for his wife, and his family.

I hope you become a man who stands tall in the face of pressure, who loves fiercely, and who leads with honor. A man whose word means something. A man whose actions speak even louder than his promises. Be the man who protects, provides, and pours life into his marriage every single day.

You weren't made for mediocrity — you were made to build something legendary.

START BUILDING.

"Unless the Lord builds the house, those who build it labor in vain."

BIBLE VAULT

N ow what exactly is a bible vault? Now, this book has laid how to get her to marry you. But does the journey stop there? Nope, it certainly doesn't. You have a give her a reminder each and every day of why she married you. So the verses from the bible below are examples and reminders to reinterate the topics discussed. They're grouped by the different focal areas.

Listening

- Proverbs 18:13 – He that answereth a matter before he heareth it, it is folly and shame unto him.

- James 1:19 – Wherefore, my beloved brethren, let every man be swift to hear, slow to speak, slow to wrath:

- Proverbs 19:20 – Hear counsel, and receive instruction, that thou mayest be wise in thy latter end.

Service

- Galatians 5:13 – For, brethren, ye have been called unto liberty; only use not liberty for an occasion to the flesh, but by love serve one another.

- Matthew 23:11 – But he that is greatest among you shall be your servant.

- Romans 12:11 – Not slothful in business; fervent in spirit; serving the Lord;

- John 13:14 – If I then, your Lord and Master, have washed your feet; ye also ought to wash one another's feet.

Accountability

- Galatians 6:5 – For every man shall bear his own burden.

- Romans 14:12 – So then every one of us shall give account of himself to God.

- 2 Corinthians 13:5 – Examine yourselves, whether ye be in the faith; prove your own selves. Know ye not your own selves, how that Jesus Christ is in you, except ye be reprobates?

- Proverbs 27:17 – Iron sharpeneth iron; so a man sharpeneththe countenance of his friend.

Love

- Ephesians 5:25 – Husbands, love your wives, even as Christ also loved the church, and gave himself for it;

- 1 John 4:7 – Beloved, let us love one another: for love is of God; and every one that loveth is born of God, and knoweth God.

- John 15:12 – This is my commandment, That ye love one another, as I have loved you.

- Romans 5:8 – But God commendeth his love toward us, in that, while we were yet sinners, Christ died for us.

- 1 Corinthians 13:4-7 – Charity suffereth long, and is kind; charity envieth not; charity vaunteth not itself, is not puffed up, doth not behave itself unseemly, seeketh not her own, is not easily provoked, thinketh no evil; rejoiceth not in iniquity, but rejoiceth in the truth; beareth all things, believeth all things, hopeth all things, endureth all things.

Grace

- 1 Peter 4:10 – As every man hath received the gift, even so minister the same one to another, as good stewards of the manifold grace of God.

- 1 Peter 3:7 – Likewise, ye husbands, dwell with them according to knowledge, giving honour unto the wife, as unto the weaker vessel, and as being heirs together of the grace of life; that your prayers be not hindered.

- 2 Corinthians 12:9 – And he said unto me, My grace is sufficient for thee: for my strength is made perfect in weakness. Most gladly therefore will I rather glory in my infirmities, that the power of Christ may rest upon me.

Consistency

- Galatians 6:9 – And let us not be weary in well doing: for in due season we shall reap, if we faint not.

- James 1:4 – But let patience have her perfect work, that ye may be perfect and entire, wanting nothing.

- Psalm 1:3 – And he shall be like a tree planted by the rivers of water, that bringeth forth his fruit in his season; his leaf also shall not wither; and whatsoever he doeth shall prosper.

Forgiveness

- Matthew 6:14 – For if ye forgive men their trespasses, your heavenly Father will also forgive you:

- Ephesians 4:32 – And be ye kind one to another, tenderhearted, forgiving one another, even as God for Christ's sake hath forgiven you.

- Colossians 3:13 – Forbearing one another, and forgiving one another, if any man have a quarrel against any: even as Christ forgave you, so also do ye.

Leadership

- Luke 22:26 – But ye shall not be so: but he that is greatest among you, let him be as the younger; and he that is chief, as he that doth serve.

- 1 Timothy 3:5 – For if a man know not how to rule his own house, how shall he take care of the church of God?

- Matthew 20:28 – Even as the Son of man came not to be ministered unto, but to minister, and to give his life a ransom for many.

- Matthew 7:12 – Therefore all things whatsoever ye would that men should do to you, do ye even so to them: for this is the law and the prophets.

Sacrifice

- Romans 12:1 – I beseech you therefore, brethren, by the mercies of God, that ye present your bodies a living sacrifice, holy, acceptable unto God, which is your reasonable service.

- John 15:13 – Greater love hath no man than this, that a man lay down his life for his friends.

- Galatians 6:2 – Bear ye one another's burdens, and so fulfil the law of Christ.

- Philippians 2:4 – Look not every man on his own things, but every man also on the things of others.

Humility

- 1 Peter 5:6 – Humble yourselves therefore under the mighty hand of God, that he may exalt you in due time.

- Philippians 2:3 – Let nothing be done through strife or vainglory; but in lowliness of mind let each esteem other better than themselves.

- James 4:6 – But he giveth more grace. Wherefore he saith, God resisteth the proud, but giveth grace unto the humble.

- Proverbs 16:18 – Pride goeth before destruction, and an haughty spirit before a fall.

- Proverbs 22:4 – By humility and the fear of the Lord are riches, and honour, and life.

Communication

Proverbs 15:1 – A soft answer turneth away wrath: but grievous words stir up anger.

Ephesians 4:29 – Let no corrupt communication proceed out of your mouth, but that which is good to the use of edifying, that it may minister grace unto the hearers.

Proverbs 16:24 – Pleasant words are as an honeycomb, sweet to the soul, and health to the bones.

Colossians 4:6 – Let your speech be alway with grace, seasoned with salt, that ye may know how ye ought to answer every man.

APPENDIX

TOOLS, REFLECTIONS, AND GROWTH GUIDES

T his appendix is your toolbox — practical challenges, exercises, and scripts designed to help you live out the principles in this book, one day and one brick at a time.

Self-Reflection & Accountability

Man in the Mirror Self-Check

Use this to examine your character and leadership each week:
- Did my words build or tear down this week?

- Did I follow through on what I said I would do?

- Did I grow in any area of weakness?

- How did I make her feel — emotionally, spiritually, practically?

- Where can I improve next week?

Reflection Questions (From Each Chapter)

Pull these out weekly for personal check-ins or date night talks.
- What brick did I lay today?

- Did I serve without keeping score?

- Did I show love in her language?

- When did I complain instead of create change?

- Where can I show more humility?

- What would it look like to show up stronger next week?

Emotional Growth & Communication

Love Language Tracker

Understand your partner's top 2 love languages:

- ___ Words of Affirmation

- ___ Acts of Service

- ___ Quality Time

- ___ Gifts

- ___ Physical Touch

List 5 specific things that speak her love language:1.2.3.4.5.

Reframing Script: Turning Complaints into Growth

Instead of: "You never help around the house."
Try saying: "Can we build a rhythm that feels fair to both of us?"
Instead of: "You don't make time for me."
Try saying: "I miss us. Can we protect time for just us this week?"
Instead of: "You always shut down."
Try saying: "I want to understand what you're feeling. Can we talk?"

Spiritual & Relational Growth

The 4 Ps Framework

Use these to overcome difficult seasons:

- **Prayer** – Start your day covering your relationship in prayer.

- **Patience** – Don't expect instant change. Growth takes time.

- **Practice** – Repeat the right actions even when it's inconvenient.

- **Persistence** – Don't give up when progress feels slow.

The Grace Challenge

Reflect on a moment where you could have shown grace but didn't. Answer the following:

- What happened?

- How did you respond?

- How might your partner have felt?

- What could you do differently next time?

Optional: Share this with your partner to build deeper trust.

7-Day Action Plan

Use this to implement daily growth after finishing the book.

Day 1: Send a meaningful affirmation text.

Day 2: Ask, "What's one thing I can take off your plate today?"

Day 3: Plan quality time without distractions.

Day 4: Pray for your partner by name.

Day 5: Do an unprompted act of service.

Day 6: Reflect and journal what you've learned so far.

Day 7: Share your biggest insight from the book with your partner.

Resources & Reading

Further books and tools to sharpen your leadership, love, and spiritual walk.

- "Chop Wood Carry Water" – Joshua Medcalf

- "The 5 Love Languages" – Gary Chapman

- "Kingdom Man" – Tony Evans

- "Wild at Heart" – John Eldredge

Reminder: Growth isn't about a finish line — it's about building one brick at a time. You have the blueprint. Now lay the first brick.

ACKNOWLEDGEMENTS

To my wife, Marina — your love has been a quiet fire that never stops burning. You've stood beside me not just as a partner, but as a source of courage, vision, and belief when I couldn't find it in myself. Thank you for standing by the man I am and pushing me toward who I'm becoming.

To my son — you've shown me what love looks like in its purest form. Your innocence, your forgiveness, your joy — they've awakened in me a deeper sense of purpose and responsibility. You remind me every day that love is not just felt, it's demonstrated.

To my parents — thank you for the example. Your enduring marriage taught me that love is a choice, that faithfulness is a muscle, and that commitment means weathering seasons with grace. Your legacy is present in every word of this book.

To my younger brother — your hunger for growth and fearless drive to break through limitations inspire me. You've always pushed boundaries not for rebellion, but for revelation. I respect the way you strive to become all that God created you to be.

To my Lord and Savior, Jesus Christ — You are the source, the standard, and the sustainer of everything good in me. You continue to shape me into the man You've called me to be. This book is evidence of Your grace, and may every page reflect Your truth and love.

About the author

Maurice Cole is a husband, father, and storyteller at heart — committed to helping men love with purpose, lead with humility, and show up for their families with consistency and strength. His journey is shaped by faith, tested by experience, and fueled by a desire to leave a legacy that lasts.

Through his writing, Maurice blends biblical truth with real-life reflection to challenge, encourage, and equip readers for the kind of love that builds homes, heals wounds, and honors God. His work has resonated with readers nationwide, earning a spot in the Top 5 on Amazon's bestseller list.

When he's not writing, Maurice is building businesses, mentoring men, playing sports, or spending time with his wife and son — the two greatest inspirations behind everything he creates.

To connect, explore bonus content, or access exclusive resources, visit:

www.LoveThatStays.com

His mission is to provide men with the insight and tools to love their wives well and lead their homes with grace. Because as Scripture says, "My people are destroyed for lack of knowledge" — and too many husbands are suffering silently without guidance.

www.ingramcontent.com/pod-product-compliance
Lightning Source LLC
Chambersburg PA
CBHW051620120626
46551CB00014B/1883